BULGARIA
1 Inch = approximately 30 miles

Bulgaria Today
THE LAND AND THE PEOPLE

Bulgaria Today

THE LAND AND THE PEOPLE

A VOYAGE OF DISCOVERY

BY

William Cary

Foreword by

JOHN HOWLAND LATHROP, D.D.

Illustrated

AN EXPOSITION—BANNER BOOK

EXPOSITION PRESS   NEW YORK

Exposition Press Inc., 386 Park Avenue South, New York 10016

FIRST EDITION

EP 43067

To all those who would make

E V E R Y Y E A R

an International Cooperation Year

FOREWORD

Just north of Greece, which has become so popular with tourists of late years, lies the least-known country of Europe. William Cary's excellent and enticing introduction to Bulgaria will certainly help to change this in these days of extensive travel. In his brief 139 pages, *Bulgaria Today: The Land and the People*, he has compacted two thousand years of history, an account of the country as it was before its revolution, its present-day system of Communism, and his personal experiences in extensive travel over a beautiful land of mountains and seashore with intimate contact with the people. He is not a Communist, but his spirit of understanding sympathy enables him to appreciate what great advances are being made in agriculture and industry. No less important is his discussion of the advance in education among a peasantry that was largely illiterate.

Fifty years ago a teacher at Robert College in Constantinople said to me, "Of all the young people who come here to study from the surrounding countries, I regard the Bulgarians as among the finest in intelligence and character."

The reader of Mr. Cary's book will be glad and grateful to him for having made for him new friends, whom he will wish to know better and whose development he will follow with warm hopes for future achievement. Many questions concerning the application of Bulgaria's new system to various phases of human life—political, social, artistic, and others—are answered with clarity and convincingness.

Give yourself the delight of reading this book! Then go to the shimmering sand beaches and loll in the sun! But also make inquiries everywhere you go, and discover that there are many patterns of living which have a variety of rewards for the human adventure.

JOHN HOWLAND LATHROP, D.D.
Minister Emeritus
Berkeley, California   *First Unitarian Church*
May 1, 1965   *Brooklyn, New York*

ACKNOWLEDGMENTS

Many interviews, discussions, and trips into the countryside and around Sofia provided the basic material for this book. In spirit, even though not individually in print (for the list would be too long), I thank each one of those editors, journalists, administrators, factory managers, physicians, engineers, artists, musicians, archaeologists, teachers, students, industrial workers, farm workers, and others who, in one way or another and always with cordiality and helpfulness, enabled me to learn more about Bulgaria.

It is a pleasure to express my special thanks and appreciation to Nevena Geliazkova, Rayna Katzarova-Kukudova, Guillermo Angelov, Mercia MacDermott, representatives of the Committee for Friendship and Cultural Relations with Foreign Countries, and representatives of Balkantourist. Likewise to my wife, who accompanied me on my second trip to Bulgaria and who has shared with me much of the pleasures and labor that have gone into the writing of this book.

The photographs, excepting "Dr. Elena and the Author" and the three following it (which are mine), were graciously furnished by State Photo Archives, Sofia.

WILLIAM CARY

CONTENTS

LIST OF ILLUSTRATIONS

(Following page 76)

On a cooperative farm
Folk dance of southwestern Bulgaria
Thracian horses, from a fresco discovered near Kazanluk
Part of the Golden Treasure of Panagyurishté
Colonnade of the Roman town of Abritus
Shilyana Radeva and her teacher
In the Valley of Roses
Fountain in the palace gardens at Balchik
Golden Sands on the Black Sea
Hotel Sirena (Siren) at Golden Sands
Fun at Sunny Beach
A room in the Hotel Globus
At the International Students' Camp, near Nessebur
Dr. Vanya Feodorova gives Lyubomir Mihailov a check-up
Dr. Elena Alexieva and the author
Engineers Katia Sankeva and Alexander Zlatarski
Stoil Dimitrov Alexiev with Velitshko Atanasov on a cooperative
    farm
Harvesting "Wisconsin maize"
Lunch hour on a cooperative farm
Slavcho Kouzev gives instruction in tree planting
Shinka Kutsinova, winner of a 1,700-meter ski race
A 1980 Olympic champion?
Soccer: Bulgaria vs. Portugal

Bulgaria Today
THE LAND AND THE PEOPLE

CHAPTER 1

"DON'T YOU TOUCH HER!"

"There are villages in the Rhodope Mountains," said Mrs.
Rayna Katzarova-Kukudova, "where for several hundred years
time stood still. There were no roads to most of those villages,
or there were only cart tracks; the people were cut off from
the rest of the world. How did I get there? By foot, often; sometimes on a horse or a mule."

Mrs. K. is head of the Folk Music Section of the Institute of
Music at the Bulgarian Academy of Sciences. A woman of
exceptional warmth and charm, she radiates enthusiasm for
life, her country, and its people. For the past thirty-five years
she has been going into remote parts of the country, gathering
folk songs, folk dances, and customs.

"Of course, you know," she continued, "that Bulgaria was
under the Turkish yoke for five hundred years—from the fourteenth to the nineteenth centuries; dark and terrible years.
Our people were persecuted in countless ways, heavily taxed,
beaten, and even killed on slight pretext. Thousands of them were
forcibly converted to Mohammedanism. Most Bulgarians tena-
ciously resisted. But the Turks carried off many of our girls, as
slaves and for harems. They also took little Bulgarian boys to
Constantinople and brought them up as Turks, to return later as
fanatical soldiers—janissaries—to kill Bulgarians. And during a
big famine in the Rhodopes the Turks brought food in front of
the starving people and said, 'We will give you this food and
more if you become Mohammedans.' Many refused. But many
finally submitted."

This went on, she told me, for several hundred years until, in
1878, Bulgaria was freed from the Turkish yoke. But even down
to about fifteen years ago there were whole villages of mountain
people who lived in degradation and superstition. They spoke

only Bulgarian, sang beautiful Bulgarian folk songs, and celebrated certain Christian festivals—yet they were Mohammedans.

These people were called Pomaks, which means "tortured ones." The women, like Turkish women, wore the long veil— the *yashmak*—which was drawn tight just above the eyes and across the nose. Their houses were dirty and unsanitary, they received practically no medical care, and infant mortality was very high. They were illiterate. Mothers would tell their daughters, "We have the Koran. That is enough for us. Learning would bring a curse upon us."

The men, when taken into the army, learned to read and write. They prayed in the mosque, but they would kill a lamb and eat it themselves, while their women and children had only a little bitter porridge or yogurt.

"In 1947," said Mrs. K., "I went with an amateur folk song and folk dance group from the town of Gotsé Delchev into such a village. We wanted to make friends with the Pomaks, to learn more about their folklore, and to help them in various ways both to preserve the best of their traditions and to get rid of those which for centuries had kept them in darkness.

"Our singers and dancers walked the twenty-odd miles to the village. They were very able, hard-working boys and girls, and they did a lot for cultural progress among the mountain people. The costumes which they had made—lovely costumes, pure Pomak—were carried in a horse-drawn cart.

"At the edge of the village was a grassy meadow, and in the meadow was a nut tree. Nearby was a little hill with a stream at the foot of it.

"In front of the nut tree our boys and girls began to dance and sing. And they acted out a wedding—a Pomak wedding, a ritual which is in no way different from a Christian wedding.

"The girl who took the part of the Pomak bride was very beautiful. And the songs that the bridesmaids and groomsmen sang were pure Bulgarian folk songs—the same songs that the Pomaks were used to singing at their weddings.

"The villagers had all turned out to see what was happening.

The men, seeing our girls in Pomak costumes, were much interested and came up close to them. But their women only looked from a distance; they sat on the slope of the little hill about eighty yards away.

"While the dancing was going on, I went among the women to speak with them and to hear their comments. They were saying: 'See how they dress the bride, just as we do! And they sing the same songs that we do!'

"At the end of the play about the wedding, the director of our group invited the village women and girls to come closer to our singers and dancers. But they didn't dare.

"'Our girls would like to talk with you,' he said, 'and to learn more about your songs and dances, costumes, and customs. And please come and tell us if some things about our costumes are wrong.'

"Little by little, some of the village women sidled up, wary and afraid. Seeing this, our girls moved forward to meet them; the boys walked over to join the Pomak men, and in two groups they began to talk with one another.

"The Pomak women were dressed in very pretty homemade costumes, but over these costumes they wore the heavy *yashmak*, which came to the ankles.

"Among these women I saw a beautiful girl of perhaps sixteen who wore a little felt cap, finely embroidered, decorated with pearls, and with silver and gold coins hanging at the rim of it over her forehead. Her white veil was partly off, and that is how I caught a glimpse of the cap with its decorations. Wanting to see it better, I put out my hand toward it. 'Please,' I said to her, 'let me see how your headdress is made.'

"But she threw herself face down upon the earth, screaming, 'Mother! Mother! I am dying!'

"The women rushed up and closed in around her, making a wall to protect her from me. 'Don't you touch her!' they cried. 'Go away from here, you spirit of the Evil One!'

"I drew back a little, quietly, and said, 'I don't want to do you any harm; I only wanted to see her headdress. And I am not of the Evil One,' I added; 'nor am I any sort of spirit.' I held out my hand toward them. 'See. Touch me. I am a woman of flesh and blood like yourselves, and I wish no harm to anyone.'

"At this point one of the Pomak men came up and explained to me that the women thought I wanted, by touching them, to put the Devil's seal on them, so that when they died the Devil would get them. They would go not to Paradise but to Hell.

"To turn their attention to more cheerful things, our boys began to dance a favorite dance of this village, which they had learned from an acquaintance—and the Pomak men began to join in the dance with them. The Pomak men then taught our boys a new dance. The music was drums and zourla—a sonorous oboe-like pipe. Soon a few of the Pomak girls began to teach our girls one of their dances with singing.

"I stood at one side, thinking what to do. If I were to try to reassure the women with a present of some sort, would they not fear contamination with the Devil?

"Then an idea came to me. I took off a white scarf which I was wearing and, in sight of the women, stepped to the stream nearby, dipped the scarf in the water, and washed it thoroughly. When I had wrung it out and shaken it, I held it out to the girl who had fallen in terror to the earth, and said, 'Won't you take my scarf?'

"No one moved.

" 'If there was any evil in me and in my scarf,' I said, 'I have now washed it all out. You can take it in safety.'

"It was the girl's mother who, after a moment, reached out and took the scarf.

"That was only seventeen years ago. About four years later, one market day, that girl of the beautiful headdress, together with several other girls from her village, came to the town of Gotsé Delchev. They stood at the door of our young people's club. It was a very attractive place, made from a store; there were books, flowers, and pictures in it. Our girls welcomed them in. Later, toward the end of this friendly visit, they exchanged presents. Then they all clasped hands, in the double and crossed handclasp which is a symbol that they were now like sisters to one another.

"Changes didn't come all at once in that mountain village, but they came. The first girl from there to go to secondary school, in a city many miles away, was cursed and was declared an outcast by the village people. Yet her father sided with her. She took off her *yashmak,* cut her hair, and studied at this school —and is now herself a teacher.

"Nowadays, most of the Bulgarian Mohammedans—we no longer call them Pomaks—live in clean and pleasant houses. The same women who once mistrusted us now say to us when we go down there: 'Come in; come and see my house!' Many of the men work on the cooperative farms, some in the forests and saw mills, some in factories, and still others in the mines. A few have even finished higher education and are in various professions.

"At first, the men wouldn't allow their women to go to a maternity home. But now practically all Bulgarian women give birth in hospitals or maternity homes. And free medical care is available in every village.

"During these past two decades," Mrs. K. concluded, "many friendly hands have been stretched out to these people and to other Bulgarians who were still living in ignorance and superstition. And one should not underestimate, either, the courage and sacrifices with which these people themselves, when once helped to see the road ahead, broke with their dark past and struggled up into a more decent, more happy way of life. People freed from bondage feel a wonderful release of new energies."

CHAPTER 2

WHY BULGARIA?

"Why did you decide to visit Bulgaria?" some people have asked me. One of them was surprised to learn that it borders on the Black Sea. "I'll have to look at a map," he said. Another, whose geography was still vaguer, inquired dubiously, "It's behind the Iron Curtain, isn't it?"

Very little is published in our country about Bulgaria, so naturally many of us are vague about it. And only a few Americans have been there, compared with the many thousands who flock to Western Europe.

I went to Bulgaria partly because it has a different kind of economy from that of Western countries, and I wanted to see what effect the big change-over of 1944 was having on the land and the people. How do their attitudes differ from ours, and what main interests do they and we have in common? Is there a "new man" emerging in Bulgaria?

Then, too, Bulgaria has been mainly agricultural and one of the least developed countries in Europe; so presumably it would show very interesting contrasts between old and new ways of life.

It is a small country. In this age when bigger is often assumed to be better, it seemed to me that a small country might be on a more comfortable human scale, and indeed more comprehensible, than a big one.

Some Polish friends of mine who had spent their vacation in Bulgaria had told me about its beautiful seacoast and mountains, its old churches and monasteries, the booming new construction, and the hospitality of its people. They had especially enjoyed Bulgaria's new resorts on the Black Sea. Their enthusiasm reminds me of a saying I heard in Sofia: "There are three kinds of Poles—those who have visited Bulgaria, those who are here now, and those who hope to come here." (Perhaps this will soon be said of the British, too, for reasons which we shall see later.)

I made two trips there: first in the summer of 1963, and again in the winter and spring of 1964. I went as a tourist, on my own, not with any organization or group. Before my first visit, I didn't know a soul there, nor a word of Bulgarian. But with English and some French and German I found that I could get along. The second time, acquaintances of the previous summer became cordial friends and made it possible for me to gather much of the material for this book.

Several times in the past few years I had visited Poland and Yugoslavia—both of them rather unorthodox members of the socialist group. Bulgaria, I had heard, was politically more orthodox. It seemed to me that if we Americans can understand and get along with the people of such a country, we should be able to understand and get along with those of the other socialist countries as well. And it is not merely desirable, it is essential, for us to learn to get along with people of the whole world. As President Lyndon Johnson put it (in his talk to the American Society of Newspaper Editors, April 17, 1964): "Today, under the shadows of atomic power, it is not rhetoric but it is truth to say that we must either love each other or we must die."

* * *

At this point we need to consider certain definitions. To many Americans socialism is some vague political setup that isn't good and we don't want it here, but which we don't have to take too seriously. Likewise, to many Americans communism is what they have in Russia and the other "Iron Curtain countries," something 100 per cent bad and a threat to "our American way of life" and "the Free World."

Webster's Dictionary is more objective: "Socialism: a system or condition of society in which the means of production are owned and controlled by the state; a stage of society in Marxist theory transitional between capitalism and communism and distinguished by unequal distribution of goods and pay according to work done."

When a citizen of Bulgaria uses the word "socialism," he, like Webster, is referring to an economic system or stage of society, and the term has for him a similar and precise meaning—a meaning widely accepted throughout most of the world. It should be remembered that what many Americans call "the communist countries" consider themselves and call themselves socialist countries. And the most important difference between socialism and communism, they say, is that under communism the distribution of goods and payments will be "to each according to his *need*." This is a very high ideal for any society, and it has not yet been achieved anywhere. Thus, accurately speaking, there are no communist countries.

I shall not attempt to deal with this vision of a hoped-for future, but shall limit myself to an account of what is actually taking place in Bulgaria today. First, however, a bit of background.

CHAPTER 3

A LOOK AT THE LAND

Bulgaria is about the size of Maine and New Hampshire together. You can fly from its capital, Sofia, near the western boundary, all the way to the Black Sea in a little over an hour. The country is about two thirds plains and rolling land, and one third mountains. When you travel by bus, car, or railroad, you find that each hour's ride brings you a different kind of landscape—broad plains, rocky gorges, pasture land, dense forests, snow-topped mountains, and little roads not on your map winding up along remote valleys. Population? Eight million, of whom one out of every ten lives in Sofia.

The Danube River, forming most of the northern frontier between Bulgaria and Rumania, provides a waterway for trade with the countries through which it flows. Parallel with this boundary and to the south of it stretches the Balkan Range from west to east, the whole length of the country between Yugoslavia and the Black Sea. Since the name "Balkans" is used also to refer to all the mountains of southeast Europe, it is convenient to call this range, as the Bulgarians do, the Stara Planina, which means Old Mountain.

It is indeed old; the wind, rain, frost, and sun of many millennia have rounded off its summits. They are now mainly grassy uplands, on which graze the sheep and cattle of cooperative farms. Below these high meadows are forests of beech and other deciduous trees.

Between the Danube River and the Stara Planina lies the undulating Danubian Plain—Bulgaria's granary. East of this plain and extending to the Black Sea is a flat, dry area known as the Dobroudja. Like the Ukrainian steppe not far to the north of it, it is a grain- and stock-raising area.

On the northern slopes of the Stara Planina are orchards,

mostly plum; on the southern slopes and in the protected valleys the main crops are grain, fruits—and roses. From the Valley of Roses comes the world-famous Bulgarian attar of roses, used in making perfume. Still farther south is the Thracian Plain, with extensive fruit orchards, vineyards, and large areas planted to cotton and vegetables.

In the extreme south and southwest are sheltered valleys where peaches, figs, cotton, peanuts, tobacco, and other crops are grown. This region is not much known to foreigners yet, but deserves to be because of its natural beauty and simple living.

The highest mountains are in the Rila and Pirin ranges in the southwest. Mount Moussala (over 9,500 feet) in the Rilas is the highest in the whole Balkan Peninsula, but not by much. Eleven peaks in the Rila and Pirin mountains are about 9,000 feet high. These are bare rock. Here and there among them, at high altitudes, are remote lakes. Below these are forests of pine and fir and, still lower, beech and oak.

Many vacationers, both Bulgarian and foreign, find the Rhodope Mountains, in the south, most inviting of all. Only two of their peaks are more than 6,000 feet high. Many of their slopes are covered with forests; and there are sunny meadows full of wildflowers, and ancient villages, some of whose houses almost touch each other in the upper stories across narrow, cobbled streets.

One more mountain—Vitosha, in Sofia's back yard, an hour's bus ride from the center of the city. Vitosha is no foothill but a real mountain. Three of its peaks are more than 6,000 feet high. It rises right out of the plain, for no apparent reason to us nongeologists unless to give pleasure to skiers in winter and to sunbathers, hikers, and weekenders in summer. Reason enough, we say.

But what about Bulgaria's other boundaries? Continuing clockwise: near Silistra, a border town on the Danube, the river curves to the northeast into Rumania, and the frontier continues overland eastward to the Black Sea. The whole eastern boundary is Black Sea coast—235 miles of it—of which more later. In the southeast is a fairly short, mostly mountainous frontier with

Turkey; then, on the south and west, long, mountainous frontiers with Greece and Yugoslavia, respectively.

Within these boundaries is a variety of climates: a moderate continental climate north of the Stara Planina range—which means that it is rather cold in winter and not very hot in summer; and a fairly mild, intermediate climate on the south side of the Stara Planina. Down near the Greek border the climate is Mediterranean—not very cold in winter, and rather hot in summer.

Among Bulgaria's many rivers, only the Danube is navigable. In the past ten or fifteen years, however, the Isker, Maritsa, Struma, and other rivers have been harnessed with dams and hydroelectric stations. These provide not only power and light but also a dependable supply of water for irrigation. Like our own Tennessee Valley Authority, they are planned for multiple use, including boating, fishing, and camping at the new-made lakes.

About 30 per cent of Bulgaria is covered with forests. This, though not nearly so much as in the days of the Thracians, Romans, and Crusaders, is still a larger percentage than in many European countries.

Iron, coal, lead, zinc, and copper—and oil—have recently been discovered in larger quantities than had been assumed. There is also a liberal amount of limestone and clay. And Bulgarians estimate that they have enough salt to last for two thousand years. That should be long enough, the way the world is going.

Mention an illness or ailment, and Bulgaria has one or more mineral springs declared to be just the thing for it. These springs have a wide range of temperature and of chemical content. Some of their medicinal properties were known in ancient times. The Romans built towns and public baths at a few of these springs, which became well known as far away as Rome. There is a town called Hissar (you'll probably drink sparkling water from there if you visit the Plovdiv region) which sometimes refers to itself as Bulgaria's oldest tourist and health resort—two thousand years old.

CHAPTER 4

A LONG STORY IN SHORT

Twenty-five hundred years ago, on the territory now known as Bulgaria, tribes of cattle-raising and metal-working people, the Thracians, had achieved a flourishing culture. Who could design and cast golden drinking goblets to match the Thracians? Or who could draw human forms of more grace and dignity than those on Thracian tombs of the fourth century B.C.? They made chariots of oak, and decorated them with bronze sculptures. And how beautifully they could paint the chariot horses—long-necked, noble steeds, with their manes blowing in the wind, and wild eyes alert in high-strung, uptossed heads!

To the Thracians (if they ever pondered such matters) it must have seemed that they had been masters in that land forever, and would forever be so. It is true that they were conquered by Philip of Macedon and his son Alexander the Great in the fourth century B.C.; but didn't they, after half a century of severe fighting, win back their independence? Not for long, though. From the second century B.C. to the first century A.D., they waged a stubborn fight against the invading Romans, and lost. The Romans subdued them with devices of advanced military engineering, and carried off many prisoners to Rome as slaves. On the Thracians' land they built cities which had forums, theaters, stadiums, and public baths. Another golden age, world without end. But this, too, was destined to pass.

In the fourth century the Roman Empire was divided into two parts, Western and Eastern, ruled from Rome and Constantinople, respectively. The territory that is now Bulgaria was included in the Eastern Roman Empire, later called Byzantium.

Around this time there were some bold nomadic tribesmen of Turkic origin who had migrated from Central Asia to the area between the Black and the Caspian seas, near the Sea of Azov.

There they formed a state headed by Khan Koubrat. These were the Proto-Bulgarians. Defeated in battle in the seventh century, some of them moved down into what is today northeastern Bulgaria. They found numerous Slavic tribes already there, and made peace with them, partly in order to defend themselves better against, and then to attack, their newest enemy, the Byzantines. The Proto-Bulgarians merged with the Slavs (and adopted the Slav tongue; there was no written Slavic language yet), and together with them set up a strong Slav-Bulgarian state, with its capital at Pliska.

Thus came into being the first Bulgarian Kingdom (681–1018). But—wars and counter-wars! In the ninth century the Byzantine emperor entered Bulgaria with a large army, took Pliska and burned it to the ground—only to be ambushed on his way home, in a pass in the Stara Planina, and himself slain.

But life in that epoch was not all fighting. Whenever there was a longish breathing space between wars, culture and the arts sprang up, even from apparently barren soil. Such sunny interludes give us a glimpse of what *could* be, if enough men had enough sense to put up their bright swords and learn to get along together without greed and suspicion.

Does it seem strange that those tough-minded warriors adopted Christianity in the ninth century as the official state religion? Perhaps not if we see that in order to bind the peasants more securely to them, and ignoring the heart of Christ's teaching and life example, they made use of the Church's doctrine of submission to authority. Where did they get their authority? They claimed that it came from God.

In the same century the Bulgarian rulers felt a need for some common written language in order to check the penetration of Byzantine influence and to strengthen the unity of their Church and thus of their own political power. They therefore welcomed the work of two learned brothers, Cyril and Methodius, who had devised a Slavic alphabet and by means of it were translating religious books into Bulgarian. In Venice, Cyril argued for church services and a literature in a Slav language, against bishops and priests who opposed him "as ravens against a falcon." They maintained that only three languages—Hebrew, Greek and Latin—were suitable for the praise of God in books. Cyril answered them: "Does not God send rain equally on all men? Does not the sun also shine on all men? Do we not all breathe the same air? And are you not ashamed to recognize only three languages, and to ordain that all other peoples and tribes shall be blind and deaf?"

The common people remained illiterate; but the time would come when, using this same alphabet, they would create their own—indeed, a revolutionary—literature. With later revisions, and known as Cyrillic, this alphabet spread from Bulgaria to Russia, and is still used in Bulgaria, the Soviet Union, and parts of Yugoslavia. Nowadays, May 24 is celebrated throughout Bulgaria as the Day of Culture and Slavonic Writing. Several years ago on that date thousands of children, teachers, and others paraded in Sofia with portraits not only of Saint Cyril and Saint Methodius but also of the Soviet cosmonaut Yuri Gagarin, who himself stood on the Georgi Dimitrov mausoleum and reviewed the procession. An eyewitness of this celebration comments: "Does the juxtaposition of two ninth-century saints and modern space travel seem a little strange? Nothing could be more appropriate, for the Soviet pennant planted on the moon and the instruments in Gagarin's space ship were all inscribed in the Cyrillic alphabet—Bulgaria's gift to civilization."

Under Tsar Simeon, in the early tenth century, practically the whole peninsula from the Adriatic to the Black Sea and down to the Aegean was brought under Bulgarian rule. Trade, crafts, and religious literature flourished. But the seeds of disintegration were there. The feudal lords lived in luxury and quarreled among themselves, while their continual wars against Byzantium left the common people impoverished and bitter. In 1014 the army of the Byzantine Emperor ambushed the Bulgarians in a mountain pass, defeated them, and, on the Emperor's orders, put out the eyes of more than fourteen thousand Bulgarian soldiers and then had them led back to their tsar, Samuïl. By the end of the eleventh century the entire "Christian" Bulgarian kingdom lay under "Christian" Byzantine rule.

Amid the continual wars carried on by the tsars and their boyars, a religious sect had arisen called the Bogomils. This sect challenged the existing order by preaching disobedience against the Church and the higher clergy as the main supports of the corrupt and war-making feudal lords, and by urging civil disobedience against the feudal state. A Bulgarian writer of the time, who opposed the Bogomils, said of them: "They think that those who work for the tsar are hateful in the eyes of the Lord, and they order every serf not to work for his master." Among the peasants and among poor people in the towns, the Bogomils built a mass movement whose influence spread far beyond the boundaries of Bulgaria. The Bogomils—like the early Christians—were persecuted without mercy. But they expressed the people's yearning for a life of peace and social justice.

The Second Bulgarian Kingdom (1185–1396), with its proud capital on the cliff tops above the Yantra River at Turnovo, had, like the First, its period of greatness. Likewise, it had the same fatal flaws: a group of rich boyars, jealous of each other's power, and a large mass of heavily taxed and exploited peasants. This time it was the Ottoman Empire that watched and waited and in 1396 bloodily conquered the disunited Second Kingdom. Thus "the Turkish yoke" was laid upon the Bulgarian neck, a yoke that was to remain there, it seemed, forever, and actually did remain for almost five hundred years.

From where could help and deliverance come? The Bulgarians were now even more heavily taxed by the Turks, who despised them and treated them brutally. Many sought refuge in the mountains, and from time to time, in local bands, made raids against Turkish outposts. Folk songs dating from the sixteenth century tell of the brave exploits of the Haiduks—forest outlaws who carried on an unequal struggle against the Turkish masters. Many, too, were the larger and more organized uprisings; but the rebels were poorly armed, inexperienced as soldiers, and without a clear program for a government if they should ever succeed in taking power. So they repeatedly met with failure. And failure meant the most barbarous reprisals.

The Bulgarians' struggle for freedom from the Turks long found favor also in Russia. Not that the Russian tsars and their supporters were imbued with democratic sentiment, but they saw in the Ottoman Empire a dangerous rival power. They wanted to smash it, gain control of Constantinople and the Straits, and develop trade with the Mediterranean area and with Western Europe.

Many Bulgarians felt the Russians to be their brothers. They were all Slavs, their languages were similar, and they had the same Orthodox religion. In the years of the Turkish yoke, some of the most widely known Bulgarian churchmen and scholars fled to Russia. Monks began to travel there and, returning, fed the hopes of the Bulgarians with tales of that huge country which had decisively defeated the Tartar hordes, some of whom had also invaded Bulgaria. Many Bulgarians longed for the day when the Russians would come and free them from the Turks. The origins of Bulgarian-Russian friendship go back five hundred years or more, and have nothing to do with Karl Marx, the Soviet Union, or communism.

By the eighteenth century, conditions were ripening toward an end of Ottoman rule in Bulgaria. Turkey, trying to expand her already huge empire, which stretched over three continents, was staggering under a crippling burden of military expenditures. European armies were improving their techniques and winning battles against Turkey. Over the years, the sultans and their army officers and agents in Bulgaria were slipping from a Spartan way of life to one of self-indulgence and unbridled luxury. The Turkish economy was ill equipped to compete favorably in the expanding European market. And among the Bulgarians a sizable middle class was developing, which wanted to expand its international trade and increase its own power, but could not do so under the Turkish yoke.

These and other developments led to a cultural renaissance in Bulgaria, reflected in romantic, freedom-seeking literature. In this period of the Bulgarian National Revival, Father Païssi, a monk of the monastery of Hilendar on Mount Athos, played an important part by writing his *Slav-Bulgarian History* (1762). It made a stirring appeal to Bulgarians to recognize their cultural heritage, to strengthen their unity, and, in the footsteps of their national heroes, to fight for freedom. With the manuscript of this small volume, which was never printed during his lifetime, Father Païssi traveled from town to town through Bulgaria, having it copied by hand. A century later his book was still exerting a strong influence on Bulgarians, who were longing and working for national liberation.

Bulgarian history in the nineteenth century is especially full of heroic struggles for freedom. Many Bulgarian patriots of various political views fought devotedly for their country against the Turks. Among them, Rakovsky and Levski are now considered by Bulgarian Communists as outstanding heroes of that period. For twenty-five years, up to his death in 1867, Georgi Rakovsky organized armed detachments, in countries bordering on Bulgaria, with which to re-enter his country and fight the Turks. Various political events and military setbacks frustrated these efforts, but through them and through his writings he helped prepare many of his countrymen to take more effective part in the revolutionary events of the next decade.

Vassil Levski realized that the Turkish yoke could never be thrown off by revolutionaries, however brave, who depended on the policies of foreign governments or on the Bulgarian well-to-do class. He also became convinced that a social revolution as well as a national revolution would be essential for the real liberation of the Bulgarian people. He argued that no monarchy would do, but that Bulgarians must fight for a democratic republic in which people of all national origins, including Turks, would have equal rights. Levski traveled from village to village disguised as anything from a monk to a Turkish policeman, organizing a network of revolutionary committees. In 1873 he was captured by the Turks and hanged.

Then came the heroic but abortive Uprising of April, 1876. It is easy today to point out its shortcomings: lack of an offensive strategy, not enough foresight, not enough practical organizing, not enough political education of enough people; lack of experience, coordination, arms and equipment. But the actual task of preparing the ground for a nationwide uprising was appallingly difficult.

Many thousands of Bulgarians—men, women, and children—were killed during the Uprising of April, 1876, and in the Turkish reprisals which followed it. The Turks massacred fifteen thousand Bulgarians in the Plovdiv region alone, including five thousand men, women, and children in the town of Batak. These reprisals were so massive and so savage that many distinguished public figures abroad—William Gladstone, Charles Darwin, Garibaldi, Victor Hugo, Leo Tolstoy, and others—made vigorous protests. But the governments of Great Britain, France, and Austria opposed the spread of Russian influence in the Balkans and therefore would do nothing against Turkey, except to see to it as their general policy that she never threatened their interests.

Those tragic times and those sacrifices are today, after nearly ninety years, still very much alive in the minds and hearts of Bulgarians. A letter from a friend describes a recent meeting held in commemoration of the Uprising. In the town of Panagyurishté (about sixty miles east of Sofia) there was

. . . a very moving memorial meeting in the main square, at which the names of those who died for freedom were read out, and the officer on duty reported that all his soldiers were "present and correct," except these. Then there was a minute's silence, and all the lights were put out (it was evening), and salutes were fired, and there was a firework display. This custom of reporting the absence of their heroes, as if they had just been killed and were our brothers, is a very typical Bulgarian one. On the following morning, there was a pageant in the square depicting the beginning of the Rising, with actors on horseback, all in the costumes of the period. After the pageant everybody went to the place deep in the mountain beech woods where the decision to hold the Rising had been taken, and a simple ceremony of remembrance was held there too.

The Uprising of April, 1876, though it failed, did help to weaken the Turkish grip on Bulgaria. And Russians, looking on from afar, said, "The time for us to strike is at hand."

While in Plovdiv, I saw an interesting cartoon in the Museum of the Revolutionary Movement; it had appeared in 1875 in an underground newspaper. The cartoon shows a flimsy cabin, marked "Turkish Empire," perched high up on four thin columns of stone. Its sides are propped up by three poles resting on territory marked "France," "Great Britain," and "Austria." In the cabin sit the Sultan and his Grand Vizier. The Grand Vizier is assuring his lord that the Empire is unshakable. Below the structure, little figures with pickaxes, labeled "Bulgarians and other Balkan peoples," are picking away at the supporting columns. This cartoon is evidently well known in Bulgaria. The English-speaking high-school girl who was showing me around Plovdiv commented that it was also reproduced in one of her schoolbooks.

Turkish rule in Bulgaria was indeed tottering, but to bring it down took the lives of many thousands of Bulgarians and Russians. Russia, which had long been trying to destroy Turkey, declared war on her in 1877. The road to Constantinople lay through Bulgaria, where she knew help from the Bulgarians was waiting. The Russian army fought bitter battles and drove the Turks out of most of Bulgaria—but did not reach Constantinople. Why not? Because at this point, Great Britain and other Western European powers which were opposed to any increase of Russia's influence in the Balkans, threatened war against her, and Russia found it necessary to make peace with Turkey.

The Russian toll of dead in that war was two hundred thousand. The Bulgarians have never forgotten this.

In the Ethnographic Museum in Sofia, my wife and I saw a curiously carved shepherd's staff which had been found neglected in a corner of a village hut in the Stara Planina. There were three snakes' heads at the top and one at the bottom. (The snake was considered an amulet to protect the flocks against wolves, and was a favorite motif in the Balkans.) In a spiral around the staff, lettering had been carved by the shepherd:

From the town of Kotel, in 1890, the 10th of September, Saturday. Unity makes strength. Today Bulgaria is free! Each brother must give his hand to his brother; we must love each other. If a man has five leva, we might like to take this money away from him, but we must not do so. If a man comes to us asking for money to buy flour, sometimes we say to him: "We have no money. Go elsewhere." And he goes to find others, to get money to buy flour and give bread to his children. And there are those who give money but demand a very high interest. One must not do that way. Now we are free!

But liberation from the yoke did not bring the freedoms that Bulgarian patriots had hoped for and fought for. Besides, many of the most unselfish and gifted of them had been killed. Bulgaria now became more than ever a center of conflicting political ambitions and intrigues, both of her own leaders and among the British, Austrians, and Turks. Each nation, jockeying for position among the others, sought its own advantage. An individual may often act unselfishly; a nation seldom does. Thus it was natural that autocratic, tsarist Russia acted in Bulgaria's interest to the extent that it was also in her own interest.

Although many Bulgarians had looked to Russia for military support in their struggle against the Turks, most Bulgarian leaders, including the most radical, had looked to the West for assistance against Russian autocracy and for patterns of freedom and democracy. America and France had gone through revolutions and had achieved some democratic institutions and attitudes that were impressive to Eastern Europeans. And England's parliamentary system and some of her laws were widely regarded as models by enlightened leaders elsewhere.

In the nineteenth century, American influence in Bulgaria was extensive, partly through missionary work and education carried on by Americans devoted to the Bulgarian people and their welfare, partly also through American political institutions and literature.

In today's Cold War atmosphere, as we know, a nation's international relations and history are often presented as all black or all white. But the fact is that Western Europe and the United States did in the nineteenth century contribute—and could today contribute—much that is constructive and valuable to Bulgaria. And contemporary Bulgaria could likewise contribute much to us of the West. Fortunately, both in Bulgaria and in the United States at present there is, it seems to me, evidence of a more flexible and fair-minded approach. What is needed now on both sides is not an uncritical defense of one's own attitudes and institutions but a readiness to listen, to take into consideration historical and cultural background and tradition, and to try to understand each other's point of view.

The Constitution of 1879 set up a monarchy, but was liberal for its time. Small, individually held farms predominated after the Liberation, because the land of the former Turkish landlords was distributed to the peasants. But soon—as has happened so often elsewhere—some landholders and businessmen became richer, while most people became poorer, and there came into being two antagonistic classes: a new middle class and the poor, many of whom became hired laborers and lived in miserable conditions. From the Liberation until World War II, there was comparatively little industry in Bulgaria, and that little consisted mainly of flour and textile mills and some fruit-processing plants; no heavy industry at all. A large proportion of this industry was operated on foreign capital, and the profits were taken out of the country.

In the last years of the century a movement for socialism appeared. Working conditions in the factories were shocking: a fourteen- to sixteen-hour day, very low wages, almost no sanitation. On the farms a movement began among the peasants which in 1899 was organized as the Agrarian Union. Of course, this was resented and fought by the Government.

The struggle between the two emerging classes continued for

decades. In 1891 the Social-Democratic Party was founded, which later developed into the Communist Party.

Early in the present century came the two Balkan Wars. In 1912 Bulgaria, Serbia, Greece, and Montenegro, in a temporary alliance, made war on Turkey and virtually destroyed the Ottoman Empire in Europe. But they immediately fell to fighting among themselves over the territorial spoils: in 1913 Bulgaria attacked her recent allies, Serbia and Greece—only to find herself ringed about by enemies; for Montenegro, Rumania and Turkey also joined the war against her. Result: a major national disaster for Bulgaria.

In these two wars, Bulgaria and Turkey alone each lost more than 150,000 in killed and wounded.

Greed, hate, shortsightedness! But have we learned, even today, the lesson which such wars—and World Wars I and II—could teach us?

In 1915, with the support of the nation's upper middle class, King Ferdinand took Bulgaria into World War I on the side of Germany and the other Central Powers. This brought economic chaos, suffering, and heavy casualties to the common people, who found themselves still being used for the benefit of the powerful and wealthy. When news of the Russian Revolution of 1917 reached them, their own longings for a government that would act in their interest soared.

In 1919 Alexander Stamboliiski, leader of the Agrarian Union, headed a government which brought some reforms for the peasants and workers, but it threatened the political and economic interests of the well-to-do. This government was overthrown by a military coup in 1923, and Stamboliiski was brutally murdered. Then came a dictatorship which, in the name of "fighting communism," cracked down on the people's renewed struggle for freedom.

In September, 1923, there was a large-scale uprising against the dictatorship. It was organized by the Communists under the leadership of Georgi Dimitrov and Vassil Kolarov. But it was crushed, and some thirty thousand Bulgarians who had thus actively challenged the Government were killed. The workers, peasants, and intellectuals had not been sufficiently united.

It must be borne in mind that there was no tradition of democratic government in Bulgaria. The people had been for five hundred years under the Turks, and many of the ablest patriots had been killed. From 1923 until the end of World War II was a period of open reaction. In 1941 King Boris signed a treaty with Hitler by which Nazi troops were quartered in Bulgaria. Soon the whole Balkan Peninsula lay under the heel of the Germans. On Hitler's demand, and against the Bulgarian people's wishes, the Government declared a "symbolical" war on Great Britain and the United States. This opened the way for retaliation later: Anglo-American bomber planes came over, dropped their loads on Sofia and other cities, and left flaming wreckage. Many people were killed or injured in these air raids, and many who escaped death were left homeless. A large part of the capital was reduced to rubble.

The Government's pro-Nazi policy was so unpopular with the people that they organized a strong partisan movement in a determined struggle against their own reactionaries. In 1942 the Fatherland Front was founded, on the initiative of Georgi Dimitrov. It was a broad organization which included mainly the Workers' Party (Communists), members of the Bulgarian Agrarian Union, and members of the Social-Democratic Party. Its aim was to overthrow the dictatorship, expel the Hitlerites from the country, and set up a People's Democratic Government. Bulgarians describe this as a government of the working class in alliance with the peasants and other democratic forces in the country. Such a government, they considered, was appropriate for the period of transition from capitalism to socialism.

In 1943 a National Liberation Army was formed, which included the partisans and those units of the Bulgarian army that had left their reactionary leaders and joined the partisans. On the eve of Liberation, in 1944, the National Liberation Army numbered 18,300. An estimated 200,000 people gave them shelter and assistance—of whom some 20,000 were shot without trial.

So strong was the people's antagonism to the Government's policy in World War II that not a single Bulgarian soldier was sent to the Eastern Front to fight against the Russians. Nor did the people allow the Government to carry out its plans to deport Bulgarian Jews, at the Nazis' demands, to extermination camps.

In August, 1944, the Fatherland Front was ready for an open, large-scale uprising. The situation was critical, partly because Bulgarian reactionaries were trying toward the end of that month to get the British and Americans to come in and "save" the country.

On September 8, Soviet Army units crossed the frontier from Rumania into Bulgaria and, aided by local Partisans, rapidly liberated one town after another. The people greeted them with flowers and the traditional gifts of bread and salt. That same night, partisans and detachments of the National Liberation Army captured the key ministries in Sofia and arrested members of the Government. Early on September 9 a new Government, organized by the Fatherland Front, was formed in the capital. In a short time its rule was established throughout the country.

Thus twice in sixty-six years a prolonged struggle by Bulgarians, aided by Russian armies, resulted in the defeat of reaction in Bulgaria and brought liberation. The date of this later Liberation—September 9, 1944—marks for Bulgarians the beginning of a new era. It is a date often on their lips today. One hears them say, "Before September 9, we had to import even nails," and "Since September 9, we have reduced infant mortality from 140 [per 1,000 live births] to 37."

On a clear morning in April, 1964, I stood on a rocky hilltop above the city of Plovdiv. Below me, in the Thracian Plain, the Maritsa River sparkled in the sunlight. Far beyond it, to the north, I could make out snow-capped peaks of the Stara Planina, forty miles away. Only in imagination could I see the Valley of Roses at the foot of them. Behind me, a few miles to the south, were the wooded slopes of the Rhodope Mountains.

Plovdiv is at a crossroads of civilizations. How often in the past had tribes and armies swarmed down from the north, or up from the south! And the shortest land route between Western Europe and the Near East lies through this same valley. Had any city been more invaded and despoiled throughout the centuries than this that lay below and around me?

I saw old houses clinging to the city's steep hillsides; the minaret of a mosque; the four-story English-Language High School at the foot of the hill; the wide Georgi Dimitrov Bridge crossing the river. On the other side were blocks of new apartment houses, the international fair grounds, the line of poplar trees at the river's edge, and miles upon miles of flat farmland now worked by cooperative farms whose long, low sheds I could make out in the distance.

Century after century, one tribe after another, one army after another—invading, conquering, despoiling—had advanced through this valley. In the fourth century B.C., it was the army of Philip of Macedon that defeated the Thracians here. Then came Romans, Goths, Huns, Slavs, Bulgarians, Byzantines. In the eleventh to thirteenth centuries alone, the city was ravaged four times by the soldiers of four Crusades, who brought death by the sword in the name of the Prince of Peace. What was left of the town, or was rebuilt, changed hands many times. Taken by the Turks in the fourteenth century, it was finally freed from them by the Russian Army in 1878.

What a different civilization our world would enjoy today if the tribes and armies that plundered their way through this valley in the past twenty-five hundred years had somehow been convinced that bringing death and destruction to others would bring a *curse* upon themselves! The world would ever since have been richer in human talents, in ancient cities, and in saner attitudes of mind and heart. The whole institution of legalized mass murder known as war would today be unthinkable.

But—today the curse *is* upon us.

As for Bulgaria, she, like many other countries, is struggling to create—at short notice and with people whose attitudes have been shaped by centuries of violence—a society whose continuance depends on precisely the opposite attitude. This is one reason why her story is significant far beyond her boundaries.

CHAPTER 5

THE BIG CHANGE-OVER

September 9, 1944, brought the end of a repressive monarchy in Bulgaria, but not the end of the war. The new Government rapidly reorganized the armed forces and included in them the Partisan units and many young volunteers. This Bulgarian Army was placed under the direction of the Soviet High Command. It fought Nazi forces in Yugoslavia and Hungary, pushed westward as far as the foothills of the Alps, and at Klagenfurt in southern Austria established contact with British troops advancing from Italy. More than thirty-one thousand Bulgarians were killed or wounded in this end-of-the-war fighting against the Nazis.

As soon as the Bulgarians had made their revolution, their new government had to move fast—not merely to keep from losing momentum but to keep from losing everything. A vacuum had been created, and men of limited horizons and unlimited self-interest tried to rush in to fill it.

A new government apparatus, a new economic structure, and new educational and public health systems had to be created amid the ruins and remnants of the old. Autocratic ministries, laws, officials, methods, and attitudes had to be replaced or reshaped. These changes had to be made quickly, before reaction both from within the country and from abroad could recover from the revolutionary blow and launch a successful counterrevolution. It is therefore natural that soon after September 9 many important events came crowding on each other's heels.

As a result of the reactionary regimes and the war, the nation's economy was in chaos. Inflation, black market, speculation in the dwindling food supplies—Bulgaria had all these. And a large proportion of the people were sick, severely undernourished, homeless.

Almost immediately, the Government encouraged the setting up of cooperative farms. The peasants who decided to join retained ownership of their lands and received a small rent for them, but the pooled holdings were cultivated in common by the whole cooperative.

At first only a few private enterprises were taken over by the Government—mainly those owned by collaborators with the Germans. No large wealthy aristocracy had developed in Bulgaria before the war; the Turks had seen to that.

In 1946 came the Land Reform Law, by which holdings in excess of fifty acres (for the dry Dobroudja region, seventy-five acres) were expropriated and distributed to landless peasants and to those with very small holdings. As a result of a referendum, Bulgaria was proclaimed a People's Republic. In elections to the National Assembly, the Workers' Party (Communists) received over half the votes. The new Government was headed by Georgi Dimitrov.

This is the Dimitrov who had been a leader of the Bulgarian anti-fascist uprising in 1923, and ten years later the hero of the Reichstag Fire trial. (On a night in February, 1933, the Nazis set fire to the Reichstag, accused the Communists of having done it, and arrested some five thousand persons. Georgi Dimitrov, who was in Germany at the time, was among those arrested. Kept in prison for six months, he was finally brought to trial in Leipzig in September. He conducted his own defense with such courage and skill, even cross-examining Goehring with devastating effect, that the trial backfired, and for lack of evidence the court had to acquit him.)

In December, 1947, a new Constitution was approved. Among other things, it makes racial discrimination punishable by law and guarantees the right of national minorities to be taught in their own language. During that same month industries, mines, banks, foreign trade, and wholesale trade within the country were taken over by the Government.

The Workers' Party, which had led the struggle against reaction and fascism for many years, and had suffered the heaviest casualties of any group during the war, grew within the first few post-war years to half a million members. In 1948 its name was changed to the Bulgarian Communist Party.

The First Five-Year Plan, launched in 1949, emphasized heavy industry and power production, and Bulgaria began to import combine harvesters, tractors, and other machinery, mainly from the Soviet Union. She began to rebuild and extend her railroads, construct shipyards and roads, and to establish an air transport system. In the same year a law was passed creating People's Councils—local administrative bodies.

Despite many hardships in this period, Bulgaria, unlike some countries after a revolution, had one distinct advantage: almost all the physicians, scientists, and other intellectuals who had had their training in the uncongenial atmosphere of reactionary rule went over to the side of the new Government. Therefore, although there were acute shortages in other fields, there were enough scientifically trained professionals to start with. Teachers were available to staff the professional and technical schools and the universities. A new public health service and a new educational system were set up, both of these free and available to all.

In 1939 Bulgaria had enough kindergartens for only 13,000 children; by 1962 enough had been provided for 309,000. In 1939 there was only one doctor for every 2,021 of the population; by 1962, there was one doctor for every 675.

Within the first decade after Liberation, schools, hospitals, libraries, museums, and theaters were built and expanded. Illiteracy was reduced almost to zero. Many amateur folk-song and folk-dance, musical and theatrical groups were formed, in small towns as well as in the cities.

Of course, there was a severe housing shortage, especially in Sofia. Most houses of the peasants were primitive and inadequate for healthful living. Therefore city apartment "complexes" and village houses in great numbers were built with Government aid. A tremendous program also was launched for building rest homes, hotels, restaurants, and entire resorts on the sea coast and in the mountains.

A professional worker told me that when Liberation came, electricity was still unknown in most of the countryside. About that time, her grandmother came to visit her in Sofia from the village where she had lived all her life. Soon after her arrival, the old lady stood at the electric light switch at the foot of the stairs and turned the upstairs light on and off. Then she crossed herself and exclaimed reverently, "Dear God, I don't know whether this is Thy doing or the Devil's—but it is good!"

Bulgarians told me that life in the countryside is much better now than before the war. Before the war, peasants hoarded money with which to buy land "some day," meanwhile depriving themselves and their families of badly needed food, clothing, and decent housing. After Liberation, they found that there was very little land for sale; most of it was pooled to form cooperative farms. So their savings were available to spend on something else. Today they are spending them on new houses, furniture, clothing, food, travel, and better living in general.

I saw no beggars anywhere. Nor any children in ragged clothes or with running noses. Today groups of men and women from farms go on excursions to the seashore or the Danube River or the mountains. And these people are not local farmers; some of them come from the most distant corners of Bulgaria. They rent a bus or ride in the trucks of their cooperative farm to see their country.

Professional and technical workers are also doing better. They are not rich, but they can get along. Some families have, in addition to an apartment in the city, a small private house or cottage in the country for vacations and weekends. A few now have cars.

In Bulgaria, as elsewhere, there are people who complain or are unhappy because they don't have more money. There is some dissatisfaction expressed about the way in which jobs and apartments are assigned; there have been complaints that "you have to know the right person." This does sometimes happen. I was told that the Communist Party has discussed this problem and has been campaigning to eliminate "pull" and favoritism.

It is not easy to make both ends meet. Bulgaria is not a rich country, and the present economic pie has to be cut into small pieces to go around. But they are making a bigger pie. Meanwhile, although wages and salaries are low, education and medical care are free; transportation, vacations, and entertainment are inexpensive; taxes and rents are very low. About 6 per cent of the average income of a working family goes for taxes; about 7 per cent for rent.

By and large, the Bulgarian people seem to me healthy, both physically and psychologically. And they are outgoing and hospitable; Bulgarian hospitality is a long-standing tradition. The Bulgarians are not spoiled, nor soft, nor decadent. They appear to know where they are going, and to have boundless energy for working toward their goals.

A teacher of English whom I met in Plovdiv told me that she had recently been the interpreter for two English-speaking Japanese engineers who were installing some Japanese sewing machines in a shirt factory. She asked them one day what impressed them most in Bulgaria. She thought they might mention a big new hydroelectric plant in the mountains, or the giant industrial complex near Sofia. But they replied without hesitation, "It's the people."

CHAPTER 6

BULGARIAN BABIES

We approached the kindergarten on the outskirts of Sofia through a gate in a high stone wall enclosing an orchard and a garden. At the right, against the wall, were some cages containing rabbits, a big rooster, and several hens. Beyond were a play house and some slides. As we drew near the main building, we saw a group of about twenty healthy and attractive three-year-olds, warmly dressed (for this was mid-March), about to start a singing and acting game on the terrace. They greeted us—my wife and me and our interpreter from the Ministry of Education—with a welcoming, high-pitched "Dober den!" ("Good day!")

Inside, we visited the various rooms with the Director, Mrs. Dechkova. How pleasant and cheerful everything was! Big colored pictures of animals, birds, and flowers; plants growing everywhere; the whole place sparkling clean and full of sunlight. This was a new school, built in 1961, and full to capacity— one hundred children.

We heard sounds of an accordion, and entered a room where a music teacher was leading a group of six-year-olds in folk songs. The children wore shorts and white T-shirts; the girls had large white bows in their hair. "Now," said the teacher, "let's have a dance." The children moved to the sides of the room, and two of the boys stepped out of the group to roll up the big rug and drag it out of the way. Then the dance started—a simple one, of course; all the youngsters knew it and clearly enjoyed it. The teacher, playing her accordion and singing, led them in the dance. Some were smiling, some were serious, but all of them—teacher and children—seemed to enjoy being there together.

The children in this kindergarten are from three to seven years old. Most of them stay there from Monday morning until

Saturday afternoon, during the whole of their parents' work week in factories or offices or at the university. Some of the children who live nearby come for the day only. If both parents are students, they pay only a few cents for a whole month. Otherwise, the cost depends on the family income, and in any case it is very little.

We went into other rooms, too. There were playrooms with dolls and a big furnished doll house, stuffed animals, building blocks, and a rocking horse. In the dormitory each small bed was identified with a picture of an animal or flower—a different one for each child. In the washrooms each child's towel was on its similarly marked peg. Every room was like a garden. In some, the whole south wall was full of growing plants, all healthy and green, many in bloom. These, like the pets outdoors, were the responsibility of the children, who took care of them each day.

In the Director's room were some dolls sitting on a window ledge. They were puppets with which she could delight a shy newcomer and charm his fears away.

As we were about to leave, we saw a slender little girl with fair hair and blue eyes—not our idea of a Bulgarian. Mrs. Dechkova spoke to her, and the child told us her name and said she was from Argentina. (Her parents were studying Slavic languages at the University.) Not to be outdone, a dark-haired and plumper Bulgarian child announced, "And I am Elena Kolicheva. I am my father's olive." The Director laughed and explained to us that this was probably because of the child's brown eyes, as dark as ripe olives.

It was the first day of March when we visited the Institute for Research in Pediatrics, in Sofia. On that day a stranger to the country would have been puzzled to see people everywhere with curious little boutonnières on their coats. These are "martinitsas" ("little Marches"), made in almost endless variety, but every martinitsa having two balls or discs, one red and one white, hanging from short threads. On the first of March you present one of these trinkets to someone you like, as a welcome to spring, a wish for your friend's health and happiness, or a way of saying "I love you." So, in the first room we entered at the Institute, it shouldn't have been surprising—but we *were* surprised—to see, instead of doctors and nurses bending over scientific reports, a ring of two-year-olds having a martinitsa party. They had just ended a game, and the nurses were pinning a martinitsa on each small left shoulder. Then two nurses brought martinitsas and pinned one on each of us. A friendly smile of welcome—who needs to speak a foreign language?

The Institute, founded in 1950, is housed in a former hospital. It is already somewhat short of space for its various departments and experimental programs. There are three teams working on problems of well children: one on psychology, one on physical aspects, and the third on nutrition. Research is conducted also in respiratory diseases, bone diseases, and in many other fields. Even as late as six years ago, about 15 per cent of Bulgarian children had rickets; but rickets, we were told, is no longer a problem.

Each research program is drawn up in consultation with the Institute's statisticians, who know the special field of medicine concerned and who recommend how large a sample should be taken, over how long a period, and with what controls.

We looked into a room open to the outside winter air where some babies, bundled up like cocoons, lay with only their faces exposed. The physician who was showing us around commented that babies whose parents keep them in a uniformly warm temperature become less resistant to disease than those who are put into the winter air for short periods, in all but very severe weather. "We do this even with babies that have pneumonia," he said, "and the results have been very good." The program is carefully regulated; the doctors and nurses watch and measure the babies' reactions in order not to overdo the treatment.

New drugs and new methods are evaluated at this Institute, and the findings are sent all over the country. The staff also holds refresher and postgraduate training courses for pediatricians, general practitioners, and trained nurses. Not much time is lost in introducing new ideas and recommendations. When, for example, a nutritional scheme has been developed, the Institute calls in pediatricians from all over Bulgaria and explains the scheme, and they all discuss it.

A team of psychologists and pediatricians have been working out a program for home care. This reaches not only mothers of children who have been in the Institute but also, through local health centers, mothers all over the country.

The Institute's section on upper respiratory diseases takes children from birth up to three years old. Some treatment with medicines is given, but more reliance is placed on a combination of treatments related to sleep, the waking hours, and nutrition. "We think that even infants," said our guide, "should have something of interest provided for them when they are awake. This stimulates and helps to develop the mind, is better physically for the baby, and forms a basis for its education."

Much work is being done there on rheumatic fever, which, we were told, accounts for about 40 per cent of the heart disease in the world. In the schools a special program is organized for children with rheumatic fever, and their work periods are less than forty-five minutes. There is some physical training; physicians and nurses also make home visits after rheumatic-fever children have been discharged from the Institute. There are indications also that certain climatic conditions help—notably, in the case of Bulgaria, on the Black Sea coast and in the valley of the Struma River.

Premature babies are brought to the Institute from all over Bulgaria. The mortality rate among premature infants is very low. Our guide told us of a baby girl brought to them very soon after the Institute started; she weighed less than two pounds. Today, she is fourteen years old and in very good health. A talented child, she has made several public appearances as a pianist.

The Government is setting up nurseries all over the country. The Director of the Institute, Dr. Stefan Kolarov, told us that about 15 per cent of Bulgarian babies are taken to such nurseries; it is planned that by 1970 provision will have been made to accommodate 50 per cent of them.

Factory and cooperative farm personnel, he said, are instructed in how to organize their own nurseries. Many cooperative farms set up temporary nurseries and kindergartens during the summer and especially at harvest time.

In April, we had occasion to walk almost every morning through the park near our hotel in the center of Sofia. It has attractive flower beds, and many large trees in which wood doves repeat their "coo, coo-coo." On sunny days the place was full of babies in their carriages, toddlers, and somewhat older children running about and playing games or riding tricycles. On the benches, keeping an eye on the youngsters, sat a considerable number of grandmothers and a few grandfathers; most mothers were away at work. The children looked healthy and played well with one another. The general atmosphere was relaxed; nobody seemed in a hurry. Old and young, each was enjoying life and springtime in his own way.

Life was certainly not like this, either for older people or for children, in Bulgaria's past. Here is part of a report by J. A. MacGahan, correspondent for the British newspaper, *The Daily News,* on Turkish reprisals after the Uprising of April 1876:

I have just seen the town of Batak with Mr. Schuyler [the American Consul in Constantinople] . . . The whole churchyard for three feet deep was festering with dead bodies partly covered—hands, legs, arms, and heads projected in ghastly confusion. I saw many little hands, heads, and feet of children of three years of age, and girls, with heads covered with beautiful hair. . . . There were 3,000 bodies in the churchyard and church. We were obliged to hold tobacco to our noses. In the school, a fine building, 200 women and children had been burnt alive. . . . A woman was sitting moaning over three small skulls with hairs clinging to them, which she had in her lap. (*Daily News,* August 7, 1876)

The above-mentioned Mr. Schuyler wrote in the same paper, on August 29, about another town, Panagyurishté: "Old men had their eyes torn out and their limbs cut off, and were then left to die, unless some more charitably disposed gave them the final thrust. Pregnant women were ripped open and the unborn babies carried triumphantly on the point of bayonet and sabre."

No wonder Dr. Kolarov, as we were leaving the Institute, had said, "We are people who are trying to forget the past, which was very hard for us; we are living in the present and looking forward to the future."

CHAPTER 7

GROWING UP IN BULGARIA

LOVE SONG

My wife and I had come by bus from Sofia into the Rila Mountains, and had spent the late afternoon walking in the cloisters of the famous Rila Monastery. For a thousand years this remote spot, ringed about with snowy peaks, had been a center of Bulgarian religious and cultural life. The present monastery—with its scores of rooms, its long arched galleries and curiously carved balconies above the courtyard—was rebuilt a little over a hundred years ago, after a fire had destroyed most of the ancient buildings.

It had been snowing, and we were glad to seek warmth and supper in the dining room of the Balkantourist Hotel, just beyond the high monastery walls. Toward one end of the dining room a cast-iron stove, with an uncommonly long smoke pipe, took the edge off the cold. There was almost no one else in the room; we were early, and this was certainly not the tourist season. One of the waitresses was playing a record on the hotel phonograph. It was—of all things—"When the Saints Go Marchin' In."

As we were enjoying some hot soup, the dining room door opened and in came about twenty-five boys and girls of high-school age, with two or three older people. Like most Bulgarian teen-agers they were soberly dressed and well mannered. The waitresses were soon busy getting them all served. Toward the end of their meal, as we had just about finished ours, one of the girls who was a little older than the others came over to our table and greeted us pleasantly with, "How are you?" Surprised and pleased, we invited her to sit down with us.

"I am Elena Mileva," she said. "I am the teacher of English in the high school in Petrich." (This is a town in the southwest corner of Bulgaria, in the valley of the Struma River; a center of fruit, vegetable, and tobacco growing.) She explained that she was twenty years old, had graduated the previous spring from the English-Language High School in Sofia—a school we had visited—and had been taking a year out to teach before entering the university. And so, she told us, she was not yet a fully qualified teacher of English. "I am rather young," she added. We held this truth to be self-evident.

Elena Mileva was petite, with black hair in energetic curls, dark eyes, and an eager, merry expression. She looked half like a child still, and reminded me of those cherubs in Italian Renaissance paintings—little heads resting on clouds. Instead of a white cloud, she had a white turtle-neck sweater.

We spoke of the contrast of very old and very new in her country. She reminded us that the southwestern part of the country, known as Bulgarian Macedonia, had remained within the Ottoman Empire not only through the Russian-Turkish War of 1877–78, but until after the Balkan War of 1912; and she said that, in fact, her own father had boyhood memories of life "under the yoke." She herself, born at about the time of the Big Change-over, had known no other environment than this one which is "building socialism."

Everything was fresh and interesting to Elena. Her life was new and bright; her country, though so old, was being renewed; her knowledge of English was newly acquired. In her use of it, a simple phrase had grace and dignity. When we mentioned that we were hoping to visit Petrich some time in the spring, she replied with charming courtesy—to us who were not only foreigners but old enough to be her grandparents—"We shall be happy to see you in Petrich." Elena, as was said of the Elizabethans, "picked her words with the dew on them."

"Would you like to hear a Bulgarian song?" she asked. "Very much!" we replied. She walked to the other end of the dining room and spoke to a girl sitting at one of the tables with some schoolmates. This girl had coppery-red hair, which fell back on to her black sweater. She sat very still, bending forward, turning a salt cellar around in her fingers. She made no sign, and the young people's talk continued.

A few minutes later a song, starting quietly, floated over the room. The talking stopped. The song, mournful and plaintive, rose and fell, sometimes with throaty reverberations like an accordion, at other times with high-pitched dragging notes like those of a Balkan bagpipe. Abruptly, as it had begun, the singing stopped. Then she sang again, two more songs, at the end of which she remained sitting quietly in her place, still absently fingering the salt cellar.

Elena Mileva brought her over to our table. "She is one of my students, but doesn't know very much English yet." We expressed our appreciation of the songs, and asked what they were about.

"The first one," replied Elena, "is a sort of Aesop's fable. The other two are about love; they are romantic and sad." She explained that, in the first song, a fly and a mosquito are in love with each other, but they fall to quarreling. They do not see a spider spinning his web. They are caught in the spider's web, and he devours them.

The second song was about a man, born in a mountain village, who has to travel far from home. He thinks of his village, his friends, and the girl he loves, and is overwhelmed with sadness that he is so far from them. "Sweetheart," he says, "when you see mist, it is only my deep sighs for you. When you see rain, don't think it is rain, it is my tears for you."

The words of the third song, by the Bulgarian poet Hristo Botev, tell of a *Haiduk*—a rebel hero—who goes forth from his hiding place in the mountains to fight for Bulgaria's freedom from the Turks. He is mortally wounded, exhausted, alone; the wolves or the enemy will soon overtake him. Lying on a bare mountain slope, he calls to an eagle to bring him water in its beak and to give him shade with its wings. "Wait a little," he says to the eagle; "I shall soon die, and then in return you shall eat my flesh and drink my blood. But carry my hand with my ring on it to my home. My mother and my wife will recognize it and will know that I have died that my country might live."

GLADLY LEARN AND GLADLY TEACH

There is a long liberal tradition in Bulgarian education. In the nineteenth century, even under Turkish rule and later under reactionary Bulgarian governments, most of the teachers were progressive. They were not the rich; they were mainly lower middle-class people. And it was partly because of the influence of such teachers that, during World War II, many of their students went to the mountains and joined the Partisans.

As much as a hundred years ago, Bulgarians in many towns and villages began to set up reading rooms which, though mainly to promote literacy and culture, sometimes grew to be also undercover centers of revolutionary activity. The tradition of reading rooms still continues; there are now about 4,500 of them, with some 850,000 members. Today many of these centers have not only libraries but also halls for concerts, plays, and lectures.

In the later years of the Turkish yoke, and down to 1944, women in many small communities, though not educated themselves, used to collect funds to send some promising local young man to a city, or even abroad, to be educated as a teacher or doctor. Then he would return and serve the community.

Today, from kindergarten through university, tuition is free. Education is at present compulsory through grammar school, and it is planned that by 1975 high-school education also will become compulsory. Fifty per cent of the high-school students and 60 per cent of the university students are receiving State aid toward their living expenses. For children who are specially gifted in any of the arts, special schools are provided. In these the Government pays not only the tuition but also a stipend for living expenses.

About 20 per cent of the State budget goes for the running expenses of the schools and universities, quite apart from construction costs. Then, too, part of the budget of each cooperative farm, large factory, and other large enterprise is set aside for education and culture. These funds are used to build and maintain kindergartens, laboratories, and study halls where children after their school classes may prepare their lessons for the next day. Some kindergartens are financed and built entirely by local cooperatives, and only the teachers' salaries are paid by the Government.

In 1944 about 27 per cent of the population were illiterate. Now nearly everyone can read and write. Those few who are still illiterate are mostly old people.

Several years ago, important changes were made in the high schools to include some required training in industrial or agricultural techniques. And for a few hours each week the students work in factories or on farms. The high schools have thus in effect become polytechnical schools. Among the subjects now taught in such schools are elementary mechanization and automation.

Bulgaria holds first place in the world in the number of pupils and students of all ages in proportion to population. About one out of every five persons of Bulgaria's eight millions is attending some educational institution. And she occupies third place among the countries of the world in the number of university students in proportion to the total population. (Per 10,000 inhabitants: U.S.S.R., 105; U.S.A., 100; Bulgaria, 96.)

"ENGLISH SPOKEN HERE"

It has been said that if you know Russian, English, and French, you can read more than half the books in the world. No doubt, this wouldn't give you much time per book; but even so, these three languages do open up a wide vista.

Russian is compulsory for Bulgarian students, and they find it rather easy. English is very popular; French and German are also widely studied; and interest in Spanish has boomed since the Cuban Revolution.

Before World War II there were several English-language high schools directed and staffed by Americans. I met a number of Bulgarian men and women who had studied at one or another of these schools. They spoke English well and remembered with pleasure the years they had spent there and their friendships with American teachers.

In Bulgaria today there are no schools run by Americans, but there are in Sofia two large English-language high schools. One of these is now being transferred to the city of Roussé for better geographical distribution. There is another in Plovdiv.

There is a French school in Sofia and one in Varna; likewise, German schools, one each in Sofia, Lovech, and Burgas; and a Russian school in Sofia.

The schools conducted in foreign languages are intended to give students a normal Bulgarian education and at the same time enable them to use these languages later in the sciences, professions, and foreign trade.

One of the teachers at the English School in Sofia which we visited told us that youngsters fourteen or fifteen years old, in this as well as in the regular high schools, are reading world literature and world history. "And since they are taught on Marxist lines," she said, "everything is part of a coherent and meaningful whole." The students, she added, have a feeling of community, of belonging, because from the first their education and their whole environment have taught them to prepare themselves for, and to help bring into being, a new society.

This English school has over seven hundred students. Admission is by competitive examination; there are not enough places in the school at present to meet the demands of students and parents. In the ordinary high schools, two or three periods a week are devoted to a foreign language; but here practically all the teaching is done in English. In their first half year the students have twenty-six hours a week of classroom instruction in English. By February they are studying elementary physics, chemistry, geography, and so forth, in that language.

Each spring the fifteen- to seventeen-year-old students, in out-of-school hours and with one of their teachers as coach, produce an English play. A few years ago they put on Shakespeare's *As You Like It*; the next year, Oscar Wilde's *The Importance of*

Being Earnest. These plays were presented in a theater in
Sofia, with costumes loaned to them—and this was a great honor
—by the National Theater. While we were there, they were re-
hearsing some scenes from various plays of Shakespeare, for the
four hundredth anniversary of his birth.

We saw the school's "language lab," with its tape recorders
and with earphones and microphone for each student, hooked
up with the control panel on the teacher's desk.

It happened that the classes we visited were being taught
by Bulgarians; we talked also with several English women who
were on the school's staff. We sat in on a first-year class which
was studying George Eliot's novel *Silas Marner.* The teachers
and students were discussing moral aspects of the main characters.

In another classroom the teacher was talking about Walt
Whitman, who, he said, was "one of the first poets in the world
to be interested in the working man." And in the textbook, I
read: "Whitman glorified the common people and the simple
everyday things of life; he defended man's rights and liberties
and preached brotherhood among all nations." The teacher read
aloud several poems, including that on the assassination of
Abraham Lincoln, "O Captain! My Captain!" It was clear that for
him and for his students, Lincoln was a world hero. In fact, they
seemed to take America's best heritage more seriously than
many Americans do.

CHECKMATE

"Let's stop in here and see these boys playing chess," I said
to the Balkantourist interpreter. She and I were walking along
one of the main streets of the city of Varna, on the Black Sea,
in the silvery 8 A.M. light, about to start on a day's trip to
some of the resorts along the coast.

A former store, with a big plate-glass window and one large
room behind it, had evidently been taken over and made into a
chess club. Inside, we met the young man who was the manager.

The room was full of tables, about twenty-five of them, inlaid with brown and yellow squares. Pairs of teen-agers brooded over the chessmen. The manager explained that most of the players were Pioneers. The Pioneers are those in the growing-up group who are organized for varied social responsibilities and pleasures. Today these young chess players were in the semi-finals of a city-wide competition. The winners would go to Sofia to play Sofia's team.

A slogan on the wall stated that "Chess playing develops in man a love of work, science, and art." Hmm! I have an inferiority complex about chess. I reflected that I had never had what it takes to play so complicated a game myself, and that this might explain why I had never shown much aptitude for work or science or art. It served me right.

As we stood there, I noticed that almost all the players were boys. And at the far side of the room sat a young girl of perhaps fifteen, alone at one of the tables, looking into a big book from time to time and then moving one of the chessmen in front of her.

"It seems to be still a man's world," I said to the interpreter, "for all the talk of equality of the sexes under socialism." (Some friends of mine in Sofia had commented that it is not easy to throw off old habits formed during five hundred years under the yoke. "Some men still act like Turks toward their women," they had said.)

"It would be a nice courtesy," I went on, "if the chess club would help that poor girl at the far side of the room—who evidently has enough interest to come here and look into a chess book—to learn at least something about the game."

The interpreter smiled, and said something to the manager. He spoke to the girl in the corner and brought her over to where we were standing. She looked up at us older people with a shy, questioning smile. The manager introduced her and said to me: "You are shaking hands with our champion girl chess player."

In my surprise and confusion, I stammered, "You mean—this

girl is the champion chess player of the entire city of Varna?"

"Varna? No," he replied. "She is the champion—in the school category, that is, up to eighteen years old—among all the girls in Bulgaria. But she can't rest on her laurels, you know; she will have to defend her title. Soon she will take part in a competition with women who are over eighteen."

"Do you play chess?" he asked me. "No? Well, it's never too late to learn."

"That's just what I was thinking," I replied. We shook hands again all around, and then I took my interpreter and myself and my gray hairs out of there.

MORE PIONEERS

The largest concert hall in Sofia was packed. Some of the men and women in the audience were dressed as if for Sunday, but most of them wore ordinary daytime clothes. A few wore sweaters, and here and there an older woman from the country-side had a shawl drawn over her head. They all looked comfort-able, intelligent, and cheerful.

On the stage, about a hundred musicians were tuning up their instruments or sitting quietly awaiting the conductor. Just one thing was strange about this scene: all the musicians in this symphony orchestra were children—from about ten to sixteen years old! The boys wore white shirts and black trousers; the girls, white blouses and black skirts; and each player had a red Pioneer scarf around his or her neck.

In strode their distinguished conductor, Vladi Simeonov, in white tie and tails. And they launched into a program of Beethoven, Bach, Vladigerov (a Bulgarian composer), and Prokofiev.

They played beautifully! Like veterans!

Beyond the cellos, at the extreme right, I could see the bass viols—but where were the players? Oh, yes, a young head stuck out below and beyond each big instrument's neck, and I could see a small left hand held high on the strings. Almost the only fair-haired player in the orchestra was a small girl with a mass of blond hair swept back into a knot and topped with a white ribbon. Her cello was about as big as she was. The first violin was a girl of perhaps thirteen. And just behind her sat a boy of about ten.

He was a handsome boy with pink cheeks, a scrubbed look, and a new haircut. His fingers flew over the strings as Beethoven's Fifth Symphony, with its insistent, ominous beat—"da-da-da-dum, da-da-da-dum, da-da-da-dum"—became rapid and complicated. He was so small that he had to sit on the edge of his chair so that one foot could touch the floor. Whenever it came time to turn the page on the music stand which he shared with the girl violinist next to him, he slipped down off the chair a bit, flipped over the page, smoothed it down with the tip of his bow, and was back there playing in an instant.

These young musicians appeared as relaxed, yet as disciplined, as any grown-up professionals. And why not? Had they not played before some of Europe's most exacting audiences—in Italy, East and West Germany, the Soviet Union, Belgium, and Austria?

Probably a third or more of them, only ten years ago, were out in the park in their perambulators! How could they have learned so much music, in the head and in the fingers, in so few young years?

And if such miracles can occur in Bulgaria, what is impossible there—or, for that matter, elsewhere, under favorable conditions? To what heights cannot the unfettered spirit of man soar?

CHAPTER 8

EUROPE'S NEWEST
VACATIONLAND

American tourists have not yet "discovered" Bulgaria. But because of its varied natural attractions—and its new hotels, restaurants, and resorts—such a discovery is likely soon. Foreign visitors are welcomed; there were more than 400,000 of them in 1963 from 107 countries—and nearly 800,000 in 1964!

Bulgarians are friendly and ready to help the visitor, and many of them speak French, German, or English.

Unless you are flying directly to a Black Sea resort, as many tourists are doing nowadays, you will probably first visit the capital. Sofia is a refreshingly quiet city. Pedestrians are at ease in most parts of it. On the main streets, it is true, there are some trolley-buses and trucks and a few taxis and private cars. At main crossings, militiamen are directing traffic, and there are now a few traffic lights. But there is almost no traffic compared to that in Paris, Rome, Vienna, London, or New York.

One is immediately impressed with the beauty of the trees, shrubbery, and beds of flowers in the parks, and their excellent maintenance. And many of Sofia's streets are well furnished with trees. The campaign for afforestation in the countryside seems to have overflowed into the city.

The streets and parks are free of litter. The Bulgarians do have cigarette and chocolate-bar wrappers, and newspapers (though these have fewer pages than ours), but I never saw any one throwing them on the street. On nearly every lamp post there is a metal trash receptacle. The streets and sidewalks are hosed down almost every day. The people take pride in their city.

Architecturally it is a city of contrasts. In the center, not far from the elaborate Alexander Nevsky Church with its gilded domes, are some massive early post-war structures: the Communist Party Building, with a star on top of it, the de luxe Hotel Balkan, and the Tsum Department Store, all severely plain in design. Not far beyond these are old worn streets, some rather shabby, whose houses survived the bombing in World War II or have been partially rebuilt. These are carry-overs from old days and old ways. New stores, new apartment houses, and offices are going up rapidly. Fifteen minutes' walk from the center of town are new apartment-house "complexes"—combinations of high and low buildings with their own shopping centers and recreation areas.

Sofia is comparatively free from advertising signs, which in so many countries plaster over, jut out from, and disfigure the buildings. There are, however, a few neon signs, announcing mainly hotels, tourist travel, and bookshops. And a few building sidewalls which have no windows (because adjoining buildings were bombed away) are being used for big advertisements of shoes and other consumer goods. I was told that they were designed by some of the country's best artists. But I don't care if they were designed by Michelangelo; it still seems to me they are unnecessary and culturally a mistake in judgment. The thousands of people who see such an advertisement shouldn't have to look at it every time they pass that place, yet they can hardly avoid it. It shouts for attention. Having lived for more than half a century in a country where we are daily assaulted by various forms of advertising, I was sorry to see even these few outdoor advertisements in socialist Bulgaria.

In winter and early spring Sofia is often chilly and gray. But when I was there in August, we had day after day of perfect weather, not unpleasantly hot, because Sofia is almost two thousand feet above sea level, the second highest capital in Europe.

Do you like music in restaurants? I could do without it. Usually it is mediocre as music and as performance, and often you have to talk loud against it to be heard, and have to strain to hear the person sitting next to you. People don't pay much attention to the music, anyway. But it is an accepted European custom, and many Bulgarian restaurants do have such music.

Excellent concerts, operas, plays, and folk-dance performances, however, are presented in Sofia. And to reach your evening's entertainment you don't need a subway (there isn't one), or a taxi. A few minutes' walk through the tree-lined streets and across a little park or two, and you are there.

Just outside Sofia is that great tamed lion of a mountain Vitosha (not so tame in winter, as I know from having struggled along its back, among hikers and skiers, in a snowstorm). With its fields, woods, sweeping views, and attractive restaurants, it is a favorite playground of Sofians and foreign tourists alike. It is one of Sofia's finest assets, and is now a national park.

After a few days in the capital, most tourists will probably head for the seacoast; but I would recommend saving part of your time for the mountains and some of the old towns and villages. Several guide books on Bulgaria, in English, are obtainable in Sofia.

If you like hiking, you can walk up mountains through beech and pine forests at Borovets, a winter and summer resort forty-five miles south of Sofia. Many people make an overnight trip from Sofia to the famous Rila Monastery, deep in the mountains. You may want to take a bus tour, or drive in your car, to Koprivshtitsa, a museum town of beautiful old houses ornamented with elaborate wood carving; then through the Valley of Roses, and on to the ancient Bulgarian capital, Turnovo. Or you can spend a day or several days on a Danube River steamer.

One spring day in Turnovo, I was having lunch in the walnut-paneled dining room of the Balkantourist Hotel, on a cliff top overlooking the winding Yantra River. Across the river was the steep-sided peninsula where the tsars and their boyars of the Second Bulgarian Kingdom once ruled. Into the dining room came about twenty Bulgarian peasant women. Some wore black dresses and black head-kerchiefs; others, thick hand-knitted white sweaters and red, blue, or green kerchiefs. Waitresses in black-

and-white uniforms and waiters in light-blue jackets brought them luncheon, topped off with bottles of apricot nectar and mocha layer cake with whipped cream. This busload of farm women, seeing their country as they never could have done in the old days, seemed as much at home in that hotel as if they owned the place; which, in a sense, they do.

Whatever you do, don't miss the Black Sea coast. There the Bulgarians are doing in ten years what took the French and Italians on their rivieras a hundred years—and are doing it better. Better, because instead of allowing a haphazard, crowded growth of individual villas, hotels, and casinos, they are planning each entire resort area. The desired number of hotels, restaurants, tourist cabins, motels, and tent sites is determined in advance. The hotels are pleasantly spaced, they are set back from the shore, and the entire long beach is open to everybody.

Many of the hotels, with their balconies, lawns, and gardens, and split-level outdoor restaurants built around old trees, are very attractive. How can so many large buildings, with all their utilities and household and kitchen equipment, have been planned, designed, and moved off the drawing boards into construction, completion, staffing, and occupation in so short a time? Surely this achievement is one of the wonders of the modern world.

There are three main resorts along the Bulgarian coast. *Drouzhba* (Friendship), six miles north of Varna, was begun in 1948. *Golden Sands,* several miles farther north, where construction started in 1956, now has about 50 hotels, 14 restaurants and 500 tourist cabins; and more are being built. *Sunny Beach,* to the south near the ancient town of Nessebur, has been open only several years. It has a present capacity of 7,000 people in hotels and bungalows, plus 1,500 in the camping area. By 1970, according to plan, it will have 25,000 beds! One of its main assets is its fine sandy beach, five miles long. In 1966, construction is to start on the fourth and largest resort, which will extend along nearly fifteen miles of coast, in the beautiful *Ropotamo River* area. Immediately behind the beach are low mountains and a forest with more or less semi-tropical vegetation. The hotels will be built among the trees. All in all, this will be perhaps the most "fabulous" resort in Bulgaria.

At these resorts are open-air theaters where plays and concerts, Bulgarian folk songs and folk dances, and similar entertainment are presented. After our return home, a Bulgarian friend wrote us:

I came to Varna about a week ago for the International Ballet Competition and am staying on for another week. It's lovely out here at Drouzhba and I am getting a real tan and rest. The parks are green and full of flowers, and the sea is absolutely wonderful, so cool and really smooth.

Now for a few words about the competition. It's going to be held here every summer. The members of the jury were most distinguished people, such as Galina Ulanova, Serge Lifar, Alicia Alonzo of Cuba, Mrs. Kennedy of Britain, Arnold Haskell of Britain, etc. The dancers were also tops, especially the Bolshoi ballet dancer Vladimir Vassiliev. You have to see him to believe that a human being can leap and turn and stand on toe the way he does and also impart meaning to his performance. He won the Grand Prix de Varna. A lovely Bulgarian dancer, Vera Kirova, who is the personification of exquisiteness and grace, won a gold medal, as did several Russians. There was a Rumanian girl who did some original interpretations, another two or three Bulgarians, some Cubans, Poles, . . .

Among the attractions of a vacation on the seacoast is the opportunity to make the acquaintance of people from all over the world—and especially from countries of both Eastern and Western Europe. Thus the cultural environment is more varied than on the French or Italian Riviera, and there is no such contrast of rich and poor.

In February, 1964, a new exchange rate for foreign tourists went into effect. Americans now receive two leva for a dollar. This makes Bulgaria one of the least expensive countries in Europe for a vacation. At the de luxe Hotel Trimontium in Plovdiv you can get beefsteak for fifty-two cents, veal cutlet with mushrooms for sixty-four cents. If you don't feel the need to dine luxuriously, but want to eat with average simplicity, you will find that a meal consisting of soup, meat, vegetable, *vin ordinaire*, and dessert will often cost you no more than a dollar.

How do you get to Bulgaria? In your own car if you have one and want to drive all the way from Western Europe and back. Or by train from Paris to Sofia. (Two days and two nights. I did it once. I'd recommend plane travel.) A number of airlines fly from Western capitals to Sofia. A Bulgarian ("TABSO") plane leaves Paris in the afternoon and reaches Sofia in mid-evening. Or, for example, you can leave New York on any Sunday or Wednesday at 9:45 P.M., by KLM jet, and arrive in Sofia, via Amsterdam, at 5:15 P.M. the next day.

My wife and I had a most interesting interview with Mr. Petko Todorov, President of the General Board of Balkantourist. He is a slender, youngish man with black hair and black mustache. Clearly he has great energy and drive. His organization is huge and many-branched: it designs, builds, equips, staffs, and operates hotels, restaurants, camp sites; arranges tours, supplies interpreters.

He told us that before the Second World War there was no organized tourist activity in his country. A number of foreigners went to small resorts on the Black Sea and to places in the mountains where there were curative mineral springs, but accommodations were modest. Real tourism started only a few years ago; in fact, large-scale construction of resorts didn't begin until 1958.

Many of the tourists are from East and West Germany; next in number are Scandinavians; then Czechs, Poles, Russians, and others. In 1963, 144,000 Bulgarians made visits abroad, mainly to other socialist countries. Their vacation money would go further there than in the West.

Balkantourist expects soon to have more individual tourism by private car. They are building more garages, gas stations, and motels. The famous international highway from Vienna to Belgrade, Sofia, and Istanbul, much traveled from Roman times, has recently been improved where needed. It is 220 miles shorter than the road that goes through Greece to Istanbul. Neither a triptych nor car insurance is required in Bulgaria now, although such insurance may be obtained at the border for a small sum.

In March, 1964, the old visa-application forms were canceled, and now a small, simple form is used, bearing the date of arrival, nationality, etc. No photograph is required. A visa is issued immediately at a Bulgarian legation or at the frontier itself, upon presentation of a valid passport and a properly filled-out border control card. The visa fee is one dollar.

Another new convenience is this: if a tourist doesn't spend all the money which he has changed into leva, he may, upon leaving the country, change back into the currency of his own country an amount up to twenty-five leva.

Balkantourist had five times as many advance bookings from West Germany for 1964 as in 1963. By early spring several hundred plane flights had already been scheduled with the biggest travel agency in West Germany. From the socialist countries, all the allotted capacity was already booked.

Mr. Todorov feels that the continued success of all Bulgaria's Black Sea resorts is assured. Here are his reasons. The season extends from May through September or even longer. The long, wide beaches have unusually fine sand, and shelve off very gradually. The sea is quiet in summer, and there is no tide nor undertow; and the coast faces east—which means that the sun is on the beach the first thing in the morning.

Most Bulgarians spend their holidays in vacation houses by the sea or in the mountains. These houses are owned by various professional and trade unions—unions of writers, teachers, artists, miners, metal workers, post-office employees, cooperative farmers, and others. A vacation there is very inexpensive and one meets one's friends there. Many vacation homes for children are provided too.

Until very recently, only a few tourists from Great Britain visited Bulgaria, but in 1964 more than 6,500 did so. And Bulgaria expects to receive about twice that number in 1965. Many of these tourists go directly from England to the Black Sea coast by charter plane, on a two weeks' "package tour." One English travel agency is offering such tours for about $130 to $200.

If England comes, can we be far behind? Yes, we can be—for several reasons. Among them, of course, is the high cost of transatlantic travel, whether you go by ship or by air. But the chartering of planes for travel abroad has greatly increased in the past few years. Perhaps some enterprising American company will soon be offering charter-plane trips from New York to Bulgaria.

CHAPTER 9

WHO OWNS WHAT

PUBLIC OWNERSHIP AND AUTOMATION

Professor Krustyu Dobrev, Director of the Economic Institute of the Bulgarian Academy of Sciences, is a rugged, homespun, battle-strengthened man in middle life. He would be equally at home lecturing on political science at the university or directing construction on a big industrial site. With him, all things are possible. I could see that if "the impossible takes a little longer," it mustn't be allowed to take *much* longer.

With us at the interview was a sociologist, Professor Zhivko Oshavkov, of the Institute of Philosophy of the Academy of Sciences. I began by asking how public ownership of the means of production, in Bulgaria, makes possible rapid and large-scale progress.

"Before 1944," said Professor Dobrev, "Bulgaria was an agrarian country and was not more developed than Greece or Turkey; but in these past twenty years we have become industrialized. In 1939 we produced forty-two kilowatt-hours of electric power per person; today one thousand per person, for our population of eight million.

"I'll give you a few essential facts. Up to the Second World War we had no machine-building plants; today we *export* machinery. England is now buying electric trucks from us. One of our engineers was there recently, and the British told him, 'Those trucks of yours are very good.' [The United States produces more electric trucks than any other country, with 30 to 40 per cent of the world's total output. And Bulgaria holds second place in this respect, with about 16 per cent of the total.]

"Before 1944 we didn't have any heavy industry. We had a few textile mills—small ones, privately owned. And we had a factory that produced toothpaste; that was our chemical industry! Today, in the chemical works in the new town of Dimitrovgrad, east of Plovdiv, where until recently there were only three small villages, there are sixty thousand people. A good part of that industrial center was built by young people, many of them teen-age brigaders. I was secretary of the Communist Party in that region, and got the construction going. Georgi Dimitrov said he thought we were moving too fast; but the people wanted it that way."

In 1963 a big chemical plant, with automation, was completed near Stara Zagora; Professor Dobrev as the Party Secretary was on that job, too. A large oil refinery has been built in Burgas; it will also produce many other chemical products. The Bulgarians have been drilling for oil near Pleven, with good results; so the Government is going to build an oil refinery and a chemical by-products plant there. And a lot of natural gas has been located, also near Pleven; a big plant will go up there.

"By doing away with private ownership of the means of production," said Professor Dobrev, "we have ended the exploitation of man by man. That's why the workers have such a keen interest in producing more. I have gone around construction sites a good deal, and have talked with workers there. They tell me: 'We're doing great things! And we're doing them for our own people!' As Marx said, when people work for themselves they can perform miracles.

"Social ownership also makes it possible for our Government to plan the development of the economy—with all its parts in due proportion. We can build first what is needed first.

"Before the war, bourgeois economists were saying that Bulgaria had to remain an agrarian country—as part of the Western capitalist system. Some economists in the West are giving the same advice today to the undeveloped countries, especially to the newly liberated countries in Africa, Asia, and Latin America.

"Getting rid of capitalist exploitation makes it possible not only to increase the people's welfare directly, but also to set apart large funds with which to build needed new industries. And it makes possible the more rational use of existing plants."

I then asked Professor Dobrev how Bulgaria plans to solve the problem of overcrowding in cities.

"During these past twenty years," he replied, "the population of our towns has increased greatly in comparison with the population of the villages. This is a desirable process, and it is planned; it is a result of the increase of industries in the towns, which need more workers. At the same time, the mechanization of agriculture makes it possible to free, for other work, farmers from the villages.

"Before the war, we had a hidden unemployment of a million people in agriculture—workers who couldn't be used there, yet who couldn't find work in the towns either, because at that time there wasn't sufficient industry. Can you imagine the misery of the people in our villages at that time?

"Now there is no unemployment, either in the villages or in the towns. And the question arises: Can the towns absorb all the workers who are not needed in agriculture? Yes, the towns can and will absorb them, because we are going to build more and more industries."

"But," I objected, "Sofia is already crowded. I understand that now a person cannot receive permission to come and live here for more than six months."

"Our Government," he said, "has decided to restrict the population of Sofia because it has grown to two and a half times its pre-war figure. You must bear in mind the big and rapid growth of industries in and around the capital. It can't go on like this. Our task is to bring about a planned distribution of industry over the whole country. The Government is going to move certain industries out of Sofia to other parts of the country, even to some villages. Only if a worker's labor is necessary may he remain in Sofia. Otherwise, every one would live in Sofia!"

Then I asked him whether he considered automation a threat or a blessing for Bulgaria.

"Four hundred years ago," he replied, "Thomas More wrote

in his *Utopia*—concerning the enclosure of farm lands by English landlords who found they could make more profit from sheep-grazing than from their tenant farmers—that 'the sheep are eating the people.' Today, in most capitalist countries, automation is eating the people.

"But automation for Bulgaria and for any other socialist country is very good. We'd like to have, right now, as much automation as America has. In our economy, automation can't lead to unemployment. Unemployment is a result not of techniques but of the social system. We want automation in order to increase production and thus increase the well-being of our people.

"When we have automation on a large scale, we'll shorten the work week. And strange as it may seem at first, the shortening of the work week with automation will be necessary even from the point of view of increasing our industrial production. Why? Because the more free time our workers have, the more of it they will use to acquire additional and higher skills.

"Automation," he continued, "requires highly qualified workers. Our Government is making great efforts to raise the qualifications of the people through the high schools, technical schools, universities, special courses, seminars, etc. Before the war, we had nine thousand students in universities; now seventy thousand. We are doing everything to prepare the whole population for the coming of automation, and for whatever other progressive techniques we may install in the future."

At this point Professor Oshavkov commented: "A few years ago, at an international conference of sociologists in Amsterdam, some American sociologists presented a report on the effects of automation in a Ford Motor plant. They showed what happened to three thousand workers who had been laid off from that plant as a result of automation there. Six months after they were laid off, about eighty per cent of them were still unemployed!

"Those sociologists said that American industrialists would find it difficult to reduce the hours of work, because they feared that the workers in their leisure time would engage in activities dangerous to the social system!

"But with us, the shortening of the work week will have the opposite effect: the workers will use part of their increased leisure time not only to increase their job qualifications, but also to take part in administering and strengthening our social system. In this way, the words of Marx will be realized that 'the wealth of a society can be measured by its leisure time.'"

HOW TO AFFORD A NEW HOUSE

There is much more private ownership in Bulgaria today, under socialism, than at any other period in her history.

Wh-what's that again? Yes; because millions of people who never before had adequate houses, food or clothing; who never had any radios, refrigerators, vacuum cleaners; who couldn't afford to buy things of comfort, convenience, or beauty, now have them.

But none of this privately owned property is *in the means of production*. A Bulgarian can't own a factory, a mine, a railroad, a bank, a theater, or a big farm or big store. Therefore he can't exploit any one's labor; he can't grow rich at the expense of others.

He can't play the stock market, nor live on dividends. Why not? There isn't any stock market, and there aren't any dividends. A friend of ours from England who was teaching at the English-Language High School in Sofia said: "I had the hardest time to get my students to understand what a dividend is. Finally, after various explanations and ways of presenting the matter, I was finally convinced that most of them did understand. But still, they could scarcely believe that by means of dividends some people actually live without working—while others do the work without much living."

Personal income taxes, like rents, come to only about 7 per cent of a family's income. In the 1964 State budget, 94 per cent of the revenue came from the State and cooperative industries, farms, and other public enterprises, and only 6 per cent from taxes levied on individuals. And even this small personal tax is on the way out, since the Government can more easily derive the needed revenue from State and cooperative enterprises.

A Bulgarian can own a small farm, or a one-man or one-family shop; he can be a private-enterprise shoemaker or barber, or produce and sell handicrafts. But he is not allowed to hire any one to work for him. Actually, most of the farmers, shopkeepers, shoemakers, barbers, and craftsmen have now joined coopera-tives; they find they can make a better living that way.

You can own your own house or apartment. About 85 per cent of the housing in cities, and almost all of it in the villages, is privately owned.

Houses, and in fact all personal property, may be sold—or bequeathed. The Inheritance Law of 1949 provides, for the first time, equal inheritance rights for men and women.

One out of every three persons in Bulgaria lives in a new house—that is, in a house built within the past ten years. How can they afford them?

Land to build a house on may be bought either from a private owner or from the Government. A family can get a loan from the local branch of the State bank for up to 40 per cent of the cost of the house. Two per cent interest is charged, and the loan is repayable in twenty or twenty-five years. Many families get a master mason to come to their house site for a day or two and show them how to make bricks out of local clay, sun-dry them, and then fire them in a pyramidal outdoor kiln made of the bricks themselves.

To build a brick house in Bulgaria is not expensive, not only because members of the family often work on it themselves, but also because there is an old tradition of mutual help. The neighbors gather, more or less as for an old-fashioned corn-husking bee. They bring some sand or cement, help lay the foundation, get the roof on and covered with tiles, help set the window frames.

The speed of house building, when I was there, had out-stripped the supply of windows; one could often see a two-story house with windows installed on the ground floor but none yet above. The whole family—often large, because traditionally in

Bulgaria grandparents live with their children and grandchildren—were temporarily living downstairs.

In the countryside, where almost everyone is a member of a cooperative farm, an alternative method of house financing and building has become popular. A construction brigade from the cooperative helps to build a member's house. The cooperative pays the brigade members and is later reimbursed by the farmer's work over a certain period.

With such help and such methods, house construction moves fast. A Bulgarian friend of ours commented: "Many whole villages have been practically rebuilt. It seems almost incredible!"

CHAPTER 10

THE CONSENT OF THE GOVERNED

IT'S A DIFFERENT SYSTEM

Since most of us in Western countries have had no experience of living under any other economic and political system than our own, we are likely to assume that a socialist government is subject to pressures from special interests much as ours is. But the nature of the government in any country results in large part from the nature of the economic system. The People's Republic of Bulgaria has a different economic system from ours. As we have seen, it is based on public ownership of the means of production, and overall economic planning by the Government.

There are no very rich people, no antagonistic social classes. Therefore there is a basic unity of interest—and this is one reason why legislative and administrative decisions can be and are made without long delays. Nobody would gain anything from filibustering. There is very little incentive for any but forthright and socially motivated legislation. Most of the members of the National Assembly (Bulgaria's Parliament) work full time in industry, farming, the arts, professions, etc. They meet in session at least twice a year, do the legislative and other business in hand, and go home.

There are two political parties in Bulgaria: the Communist Party (with 528,000 members) and the Agrarian Union (with about 120,000). Todor Zhivkov, First Secretary of the Central Committee of the Communist Party, is the country's Prime Minister.

Georgi Traikov, Secretary of the Agrarian Union, of which he has been a member since 1919, is President of the Presidium of the National Assembly. The Agrarian Union, while working for the over-all interests of the country, represents especially the farming population, most of whom today are members of the cooperative and State farms.

These two parties agree on basic principles, such as co-operative-farm organization and foreign policy. Minor differences are settled by discussion.

There is also the Fatherland Front, which is not a political party but a large mass organization. About two thirds of the adult population are members. It was formed during World War II, and has a multitude of political, educational, and cultural activities. It proposes candidates for election and holds public meetings to discuss their qualifications; promotes competitions for well kept, attractive dwelling houses; organizes reading clubs and courses for young mothers; and sets up control commissions which check on local weights and measures to help the Government's weights-and-measures department. It works to foster the growth of grass-roots democracy and helps the people take a larger part in the government of the country. The Fatherland Front does much to insure that those who come into public office are competent.

The main way in which the people express their views about candidates for office, and about persons already in office, is at public meetings organized by their local Fatherland Front. At pre-election meetings, the Fatherland Front presents a slate of candidates for the local People's Councils, the District Councils, and the National Assembly. Elections are held on the basis of equal and direct voting, by secret ballot. Bulgarian citizens eighteen years old and older, irrespective of sex, race, religion, national origin, or property status, have the right to vote and to be elected. They may either vote for candidates on the Fatherland Front list or cross out those names and write in others. But since the Fatherland Front is composed of most of the voters throughout the country and represents the views of most of its members—it has no economic or political reason to do otherwise—it is natural that almost all the votes go to Fatherland Front candidates.

WHO MAKES THE LAWS?

There is only one law-making body in the country, and that is the National Assembly. In addition to passing laws, it considers and votes on the Government economic plans and the national budget, says how much money shall be spent for what, levies taxes, and decides questions of domestic and foreign policy. It sets up the various Government departments and determines their functions; elects the Chief Prosecutor (Attorney General) and the members of the Supreme Court.

It also elects its own Presidium, which has extensive powers but is responsible to the National Assembly. The Presidium is a sort of collective president of the nation. It appoints diplomatic and consular representatives, and arranges for the holding of elections.

At present the National Assembly has 321 members, elected for a four-year term, one member for every 25,000 of the population. Of these members, 18 per cent come from industry, construction, and transport—as workers, engineers, technicians, and heads of enterprises; and 16 per cent work in agriculture. Thus a third of the members are from the production sector of the economy.

Fifty-two per cent are in Government administration, or hold office in one of the two political parties, or work in public health or some other of the social services. About 10 per cent are scientists, artists, or other cultural workers. (At present, of thirty-one such members, ten are members of, and two are candidates for, the Academy of Sciences; eight are professors, three are artists, two are writers, two are journalists, one is a composer.) About 4 per cent are military people.

There are sixty-five women in the present National Assembly. Among them are engineers, agricultural scientists, and team leaders in industry and farming. One of these, Olga Naidenova, is an engineer in the same textile mill where she started as an unskilled worker. She commented, "Long ago I thought my future was definitely cut out for me. I was to work as a maid in other people's houses." Another, Boika Kissimova, was the first Bulgarian-Mohammedan woman in her village to throw off the *yashmak* and study at the university. Donka Panayotova, thirty years old, is a former peasant girl who obtained exceptionally high yields of wheat. She is a graduate of the School of Agriculture in Sofia, and works as agronomist on a cooperative farm.

Of the total 321 members, 307 are Bulgarians, 13 are of Turkish origin, and one is a Jew.

As for political distribution, 61 per cent are Communists, 25 per cent are members of the Agrarian Union, 6.5 per cent nonparty people, and about 7 per cent members of the Comsomol (Communist youth) organization.

The National Assembly considered the State Budget for 1964 and voted to devote about 79 per cent of it to the national economy and to social and cultural work. To national defense— 9 per cent.

The main work of preparing legislation is done by the Parliamentary Commissions, elected by the National Assembly. These include, among others, Commissions on the State economic plan and budget; on industry; on construction and town planning; on public health, labor, and welfare; on education and culture; on agriculture and forestry; and on foreign affairs. The appropriate Commission discusses and introduces each bill at a meeting of the National Assembly.

"This system," says Georgi Koulishev, a non-party member of the National Assembly and Vice-President of its Presidium, "brings much better results than the endless, unprincipled, and idle arguments which are often held in Western parliaments."

CRITICISM FROM WITHIN

Unlike Poland and Yugoslavia, Bulgaria is politically one of the more orthodox of the socialist countries. Her foreign policy is similar to that of the Soviet Union; the newspapers on the stands express almost exclusively the point of view of her own and foreign Communist parties.

But I found a good deal of fresh and individual thinking among

Bulgarians with whom I talked. It is significant that most of them felt confident that if and when Cold War tensions are eased, a more informed and relaxed attitude toward their country will develop in the West, and that then certain of their present restrictions in reading matter, films, and so on, will disappear.

Probably the citizens of any country would rather say what they don't like about it than have foreigners tell them what is wrong. This is only natural, although of course a key to learning and a sign of maturity is the ability to accept criticism and profit by it, no matter where it comes from.

Certainly a Cold War atmosphere, in East or West, does not promote objective discussion of what is happening under different political systems. The Bulgarians have suffered so much in their long struggle for a government which would act in their interests that now that they feel that they have such a government they naturally would prefer any criticism of it from outside to be informed and constructive.

On the other hand, within Bulgaria frequent criticism of the way some things are being done is publicly voiced by journalists, in letters to the editor, in programs on the radio and television, and by political leaders.

A letter to the editor will complain about the quality of the bread during a wheat shortage, or about favoritism in allotting jobs or apartments. In the movie theaters a film will show a cooperative farmyard, for example, where machines are being neglected and allowed to rust. The film gives the name and location of the farm and the name of its chairman. Every week there is a newsreel called "Our Satire," which is critical of some aspect of current Bulgarian life, such as red tape and bureaucracy. There is also a weekly satirical newspaper called the "Hornet," which makes stinging points about individual or organizational shortcomings. And there is a newspaper column called "Along the Trail of Our Criticism," which tells what happened as a result of criticisms previously published; that is, whether and in what way a bad condition or attitude was changed.

ON A COOPERATIVE FARM
Is the wheat ripe for harvest?

FOLK DANCE OF SOUTHWESTERN BULGARIA

THRACIAN HORSES
From a fresco of the 3d or 4th century B.C., in a
Thracian tomb discovered near Kazanluk. *(Chapter 4.)*

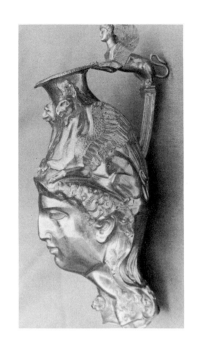

PART OF THE GOLDEN TREASURE
OF PANAGYURISHTÉ
One held the goblet high and let the
wine pour into his mouth from the
small hole in the neck. *(Chapter 15.)*

GRANDEUR THAT WAS ROME'S
Colonnade of the Roman town of Abritus,
in northeastern Bulgaria. *(Chapter 15.)*

GLADLY LEARN AND GLADLY TEACH
Shilyana Radeva and her teacher.

FOUNTAIN IN THE PALACE GARDENS AT BALCHIK
Formerly the summer home of Queen Marie of Rumania,
on the Black Sea, now a favorite spot for tourists.

IN THE VALLEY OF ROSES
(Chapter 14.)

GOLDEN SANDS ON THE BLACK SEA
(Chapter 8.)

HOTEL SIRENA (SIREN) AT GOLDEN SANDS

FUN AT SUNNY BEACH
In the background is the Hotel Globus. The beach,
of fine sand, is five miles long. *(Chapter 8.)*

AT THE INTERNATIONAL STUDENTS' CAMP
Near Nessebur on the Black Sea. These young people
are from Algeria, Italy and the Soviet Union.

A ROOM IN THE HOTEL GLOBUS

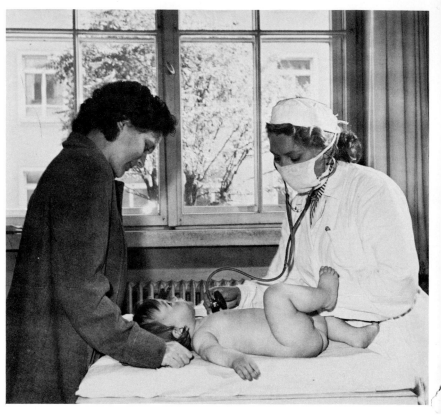

PREVENTIVE MEDICINE
Dr. Vanya Feodorova gives Lyubomir Mihailov a check-up.

ENGINEERS KATIA SANKEVA
AND ALEXANDER ZLATARSKI
(Chapter 13.)

DR. ELENA ALEXIEVA AND THE AUTHOR
"Bulgarian psychiatrists respect Freud . . . but . . ." *(Chapter 11.)*

CHAIRMAN OF 14,000 ACRES
Stoil Dimitrov Alexiev *(left)* with Velitshko Atanasov,
a guard on the cooperative farm. *(Chapter 14.)*

LUNCH HOUR ON A COOPERATIVE FARM

HARVESTING "WISCONSIN MAIZE" *(Chapter 14.)*

RECLAIMING THE LAND
Forester Slavcho Kouzev gives instruction
in tree planting. *(Chapter 14.)*

A 1980 OLYMPIC CHAMPION?

WINNER OF A 1,700-METER SKI RACE
Shinka Kutsinova at Borovets.

SOCCER: BULGARIA VS. PORTUGAL
The player in the center is Portuguese,
the other two are Bulgarian.

Some of the most trenchant criticisms are made by Prime Minister Zhivkov. To read them out of context, one might think that the socialist Government, which is only twenty years old, is doing very badly, and that the public-ownership economy is falling apart. Actually, the head of the Communist Party and of the Government is only exposing some deficiencies in order that they may be corrected.

The following passages are taken from Todor Zhivkov, *Speeches, Reports, Articles, 1962–June 1963* (Foreign Languages Press, Sofia, 1963):

Many enterprises already produce high-grade and beautiful consumer goods, which may please even the most exacting aesthetic taste. Such goods are a delight. But at the same time, we cannot but admit that a number of our enterprises also produce low-grade consumer goods. It is legitimate to ask the managers, Party leadership, chief engineers, specialists and master workers, designers, constructors, model-makers and production teams of these enterprises: "How long, dear producers, are you going to produce low-grade goods?" Hasn't the time come to tell them: "Stop producing shoddy goods and improve your output, give us modern high-grade goods, which will meet the growing needs of the Bulgarian people." (Page 27)

Heroes are emerging from among this people, new men, conscientious and disciplined builders of the new life. But it would be erroneous not to see that together with them, together with these inspired builders there are people who systematically infringe the norms of our society, undermine labor discipline, and care not a penny for plan fulfillment or for the prestige of their enterprise or farm. People who, like the flying Dutchman or cuckoos, shift from enterprise to enterprise, from town to town, carrying their petty bourgeois habits with them . . . Such a fellow should be asked, "Now, old boy, where do you come from, why have you left your job, and why have you come to our enterprise?" (Page 33)

[Some managers of enterprises, farms, and departments] sometimes show a lack of concern for the workers, refuse to grant their legitimate demands in all sorts of ways, and fail to respect the legitimate rights of the working people, deprive them of these rights, and do not care a hoot for human beings. Some of them only look to the meters, the grams, and the kilograms and do not see men, nor do they take the most elementary care of them. (Page 34)

I was in the Rhodopes not long ago. They are famed for their scenic beauty; moreover, the Rhodope people sing beautifully. All this is well and good, but they don't fulfill the plan for non-ferrous metallurgy. So I told them: "It is really beautiful out here, the Rhodopes are just wonderful. It is pleasant to hear you sing so well. All honor to the scenic beauty of the Rhodopes and to your singing talent. But you don't fulfill the plan for non-ferrous metallurgy." (Page 95)

For centuries a whole people had been disdained and cruelly exploited by successive governments. It is indeed difficult to transform such a people into socially responsible builders of a new society! And in so short a time! But their new socialist environment—with a prod now and then such as those quoted above—is doing exactly this.

CHAPTER 11

IN SICKNESS AND IN HEALTH

HERE—TAKE THIS

Bulgarians like to tell you about an herb doctor who practiced folk medicine many years ago. One day a peasant came to him complaining of stomach ache. The herb doctor brewed a potion and gave it to him. The next day, the peasant returned to say that he was completely well. The herb doctor wrote in his notebook: "This herb cures stomach ache." A few weeks later a priest came to him, likewise complaining of stomach ache. The herb doctor brewed a potion of the same kind and gave it to him. But the next day, the priest died. The herb doctor then added in his notebook: "Not good for priests."

And today? Here are a few medical facts. Today in Bulgaria the death rate of women in childbirth is lower than in any other country in the world. In 1944, Bulgaria's infant-mortality rate (deaths during the first year per 1,000 children born alive) was 140; now it is 37.3. In 1944, almost no births took place in hospitals; in fact, nearly 70 per cent of the births received no medical assistance whatever. Today about 98 per cent of all Bulgarian babies are born in hospitals or maternity homes.

The general death rate dropped from 13.6 per 1,000 in 1944 to 8.1 in 1963. This is the fourth lowest general death rate in Europe (only Iceland, Holland, and Poland have lower rates), and is lower than those of the U.S.A. (9.3 in 1963), Great Britain, and Sweden.

Bulgaria holds sixth place in the world for the number of doctors in proportion to population. She has one doctor for every 624 persons. (France has one doctor for about every 1,000; Turkey, one for about every 3,600.)

ALL IN TWENTY YEARS

The World Health Organization published in 1961 a report of a study tour made under its auspices in 1960, on rural health services in Bulgaria. It says:

The guiding principles of Bulgarian health policy are these: 1) Public health is a work of the State; 2) The development of public health is based on preserving good health and preventing the spread of disease; and 3) The population take an active part in building public health through organizations such as the trade unions, the Bulgarian Red Cross, the Fatherland Front, etc. . . .
Every doctor, whatever his specialty, even the surgeon, is required to take part in the health education of the population; that is, education in how to keep well and how to prevent the spread of disease.
Unbelievable as it might seem, in certain rural areas infant mortality has dropped to zero—a figure particularly eloquent, and one which, in this field, is of basic importance because, whatever may be the general percentage of infant mortality, for a mother when she loses her child it is always 100 per cent.

In Sofia I had an interview with Dr. Mincho Nikov, Director of the Treatment and Prevention Department in the Ministry of Public Health. He told me that right after World War II there were only about 3,000 physicians in the whole of Bulgaria. Many of these had had their training in France, Germany, Austria, or Czechoslovakia. There was only one medical school; it was in Sofia, and graduated about 40 students a year. At present Bulgaria has about 15,000 physicians, most of them trained in their own country. The three medical schools (in Sofia, Plovdiv, and Varna) now graduate a total of 400 to 500 students each year.

When a medical student has finished his formal academic training and his year of internship, he is required to spend three years practicing medicine in the villages. (An exception to this rule is made for the student who, after internship, qualifies by an examination to enter directly some medical specialty, such as surgery or immunology.)

Practicing physicians are required to read medical literature in a foreign language—either English, French, German, or Russian—and to submit reports on such reading. Language courses are held in hospitals, and are broadcast on the radio, to help prepare them in these languages.

Before the war, half a million of the people had malaria. The Bulgarians have drained the swamps and taken various other measures—and have eliminated malaria. There were 200,000 cases of tuberculosis; a large part of the population had dysentery; many young children died of scarlet fever or diphtheria; many were crippled by poliomyelitis. In the past twenty years, the Bulgarians have reduced these and other diseases to a small fraction of what they were. Inoculation against smallpox, tetanus, whooping cough, diphtheria, tuberculosis, and poliomyelitis is compulsory. In 1960, two million children were inoculated with the live polio vaccine, taken orally, developed by Soviet Academician Choumakov. This vaccine is now administered to all newborn infants. There had been 1,065 new cases of polio in 1957; in 1963, there were only four. Typhoid fever and venereal disease also have been practically eliminated.

There are now eighteen nursing schools and schools for laboratory and X-ray technicians, compared with only two before the war. In 1939 there were some 2,000 trained nurses and medical technicians; now, 30,000.

Natural childbirth was introduced in Bulgaria in 1950. By 1963, said Dr. Nikov, 70 per cent af all pregnant women in the cities were receiving training in this method, and 50 per cent in the villages.

Medical examinations, laboratory tests, treatment, surgery, hospital stay, are all free. Medicines and medical supplies, when administered in a hospital or clinic, are likewise free. If, however, a patient needs medicine outside the hospital, or for example, a pair of eyeglasses, he pays for them. The prices are low, because the Government itself makes or imports the items, sets the prices, and makes no profit. Actually, they are sold below cost, on the theory that good health for the whole population is one of the best investments a nation can make.

A Bulgarian friend of ours had recently spent three weeks in hospital, had had about sixty injections "and a lot of pills and antibiotics, and didn't pay a cent." While there, she received 80 per cent of her salary. "Furthermore," she said, "it seemed to me that the doctors, who are paid a regular monthly salary by the Government, are not interested in getting rich. The selfish person is the exception."

Medicines are on sale at 2,500 pharmacies— five times as many as in 1944. Bulgaria now manufactures about 900 different medicines, including antibiotics, and many kinds of vaccines and serums, some of which are now exported. Bulgarian diphtheria and tetanus serums, for example, are used in India, Cuba, and Syria.

About twelve years ago a medical research scientist, Dr. Dimiter Paskov, derived from a wild plant, the snowdrop, a medicine now known as "Nivalin," which in a somewhat different form had long been used in folk medicine. It is very effective in severe cases of polio, in certain injuries to the nervous system, in bronchial asthma, glaucoma, and for helping to bring patients out of anaesthesia with minimal side effects. It has recently been exported to France, Italy, the Near East, South America, and Japan.

The Ministry of Health emphasizes that apart from all these recent developments in medicine, "for man's health it is the social environment that is of decisive importance." This environment now includes a great number of new, healthful dwelling houses, good water supply, labor legislation, improved nutrition, widespread physical culture, the freeing of women from much fatiguing housework, and the countrywide campaign for health education. About 30 per cent of the population have taken courses in elementary health measures offered by the Bulgarian Red Cross. And there is a big network of sanatariums, rest homes, school-lunch programs, crèches, and kindergartens.

All these things cost a lot of money. About 10 per cent of the national budget is allocated for public health. (As we have seen, 9 per cent goes for defense.)

What about "senior citizens"? The Government pension system covers practically everybody. (Private farmers—there are now only about twenty thousand of them—are given pensions under the same conditions as cooperative farmers.) A person becomes eligible for a retirement pension after fifteen to twenty-five years of work, depending on the nature of the work; men at age fifty to sixty, women at age forty-five to fifty-five.

TOBACCO WITHOUT NICOTINE

There are said to be 750,000,000 smokers in the world. Many of them have impaired health because of too much smoking, but—in spite of their doctors' advice and various published reports on the relation between smoking and cancer—they somehow can't give up the habit. Such people may be interested to know that a team of research workers at the Plant Growing Institute of the Academy of Agricultural Sciences, in Sofia, after three years of experimentation (1960–63), has produced two kinds of tobacco that don't contain any nicotine.

One of these, called *Atrotobacco,* was produced by grafting tobacco scions on the wild thorn-apple. It has the aroma and flavor of tobacco, but doesn't contain the harmful nicotine alkaloid. Instead, three medicinal alkaloids are accumulated in its leaves. Smoking Atrotobacco is said to be helpful in some cases of ulcers and bronchial asthma.

Tobacco scions were also grafted on tomato stock. The tomato is not an alkaloid-producing plant: its roots do not synthesize nicotine or any other alkaloid. The resulting plant, however, which is called *Neutrotobacco,* has likewise the characteristic aroma and taste of regular tobacco.

The researchers found that either of these two nicotine-free tobaccos requires two and a half times as much labor to produce as other tobacco does. But one of the creators of the new varieties, the agronomist Lyubomir Shoukarev, comments: "When we remember that the tobacco contained in a pack of cigarettes accounts for only 20 per cent of the total price, and the other 80 per cent represents processing, administrative and handling expenses, and the State excise tax, it is clear that Atrotobacco and Neutrotobacco will be available to the consumer for a price not much above that of ordinary cigarettes."

As these lines are being written, word comes that a Bulgarian scientist, Strashimir Ingilizov, has developed a preparation known as Tabex which enables smokers to give up tobacco. It is made from the yellow-flowered shrub, *Cytisus laburnum,* and is said to be completely harmless. I was told that most of those who start taking Tabex stop smoking on the second or third day. Its production has been authorized by the Bulgarian public health authorities, and presumably it will soon be on the market.

LONG LIVE YOGURT!

Some years ago a Swedish university student went to Bulgaria, along with other young people from many countries, to help build a big dam for a hydroelectric plant. Bulgarian friends on the project told him that yogurt was what made their people so strong, indeed what made some of them live to be a hundred years old. One day he and his friends were invited to a peasant wedding in a nearby village. The bride's mother set before him a big bowl of yogurt. He found it delicious! "You can't get this in Sweden," he thought to himself, and he didn't object when she filled his bowl again. He managed to eat it—but enough was enough. At the offer of a third bowlful, he smiled and shook his head.

Now, in Bulgaria, to nod your head means "No," and to shake your head from side to side means "Yes." So his flattered hostess filled his bowl a third time. He struggled through it, but he felt a cold sweat on his forehead. He thought his eyes probably weren't really bulging; they only felt that way. The good woman approached with more yogurt. He vigorously shook his head. She filled his bowl a fourth time.

It is not recorded how he managed to escape from this festive scene. But on the way back to the work camp, he said to his Bulgarian friends: "Maybe yogurt prolongs the life of Bulgarians, but it nearly put an end to mine!"

SORE THROAT AND PSYCHIATRY
UNDER SOCIALISM

A knock on the door of our hotel room in Sofia. My wife went to answer it while I sat there in bed wishing I didn't have this sore throat. In came our hearty friend Guillermo Angelov, a Bulgarian journalist whom I had met on the beach near Varna the previous summer. He speaks English well, having studied before the war at a school run by Americans near Sofia. I had phoned him that I really ought to see a doctor, and that I hoped it might be one who, in the same visit, would be able to tell me a little about psychiatry in Bulgaria.

Yes, he had brought a physician with him—an attractive young woman, Dr. Elena Alexieva. She seemed a healthy outdoor type; perhaps a good skier. She had a mass of black hair and wore a light brown sweater. At the upper left-hand corner of the sweater was pinned a little red and white "martinitsa," that trinket which people give each other, like a valentine, on the first of March. She put her black doctor's satchel on the desk and sat waiting while I stated my complaint and Guillermo translated it.

She then took out the stethoscope, blood-pressure kit, and notebook from her satchel, and within a few minutes had inspected my throat, taken my pulse, listened to my heart beat, stethoscoped my chest, ascertained that my appendix was inactive, and found that my blood pressure was normal. She wrote out prescriptions for a drug-store remedy for sore throat, and for some vitamin pills in view of the winter weather we were having and the difference in diet from what I had been used to.

"To get at this throat infection in a more basic way," she said, "I would suggest that you go to the hospital for a laboratory test." (This I did several days later.) She then said that in the time remaining before she had to leave for the hospital she would be glad to answer my questions about psychiatry in her country.

I began by saying that an increasing number of people in the

United States are interested in the relation between an economic system and the mental health of the people who live under it. I added that I'd like to know the main causes of neuroses, and of the need for psychiatry, in Bulgaria.

"We should make a distinction," she replied, "between a neurosis and a condition that calls for psychiatric treatment. A neurosis is a functional disturbance of the nervous system which doesn't cause any organic effect on the brain. It is expressed, for example, by disturbance of one's sleep, or one becomes easily tired; and there are other bodily sensations. These are neuroses."

"In general, what causes them?" I asked. "What is worrying these people?"

"We find that most neuroses," said Dr. Alexieva, "are due to conflicts in the family environment. In Bulgaria, as perhaps you know, the members of three generations of a family often live together in the same house or apartment. They are likely to have very different ideas about food, health, behavior—all sorts of things. And neuroses sometimes develop from conflict in such an environment. Occasionally—but this is more rare—a neurosis results from the work situation; for example, when there are new techniques which the worker cannot adjust to.

"Some people who have had heart trouble for a long time develop a neurosis because of it. The treatment of a neurosis is complex. On the one hand, the aim is to calm the nervous system; on the other hand, to strengthen the patient's general health. When the neurosis is due to conditions of work in a factory or elsewhere, the patient is released from his work environment; he is sent to a balneosanatorium, where he is given various treatments including physiotherapy.

"Now as to psychiatric treatment: the patient goes to a doctor in the polyclinic in the district where he lives. He is given a physical check-up. If found to be physically normal, he is referred to a neurologist in the same polyclinic.

"As in other countries, about 60 per cent of the psychiatric cases in Bulgaria are schizophrenic. Up to about eight years ago, 'schizophrenia' was a blanket diagnosis. Persecution complex or hallucinations were considered to be schizophrenic. But today, with improved methods, it is possible to differentiate the schizophrenic case from those with similar symptoms. This is very important, because the latter can be treated more easily and successfully, while people with a true schizophrenia are likely to end up with a deterioration of their personality."

She said that recently, with the use of neuroplegic medications, such as "Largactil"—in fact, with a whole series of medicines, which are continually being improved—Bulgarian physicians have been able to retard the development of schizophrenia, and sometimes even to cure it.

A patient may be under treatment for one or two years. Then he goes home and is under the care of a psychiatrist at the psychoneurological clinic in his district. Everyone who has been a patient in a mental hospital is subject to check-ups from time to time over a period of not less than five years.

The patient receives his salary even if he is in the hospital for as long as two years; but if it is clear that he will become disabled, he is pensioned. And periodically he goes before a commission for reappraisal. Then he may be given a regular job, or some other work that he can do; or he is retrained. Occupational therapy is widely used. It is a part of every mental hospital. The patient does what work he is able to do, and is paid for what he does.

I asked Dr. Alexieva how Bulgarian psychiatrists regard the theories of Freud.

"There is a rational kernel in Freud's theories," she replied, "but it is not in his Oedipus complex, libido, death wish, and so on. His theories may have some application in some cases, but we can't explain all psychological illnesses by them. Bulgarian psychiatrists respect Freud as a man who contributed much in the field, who has given perhaps the best clinical descriptions of various mental illnesses."

My next question was, "What effects has the Bulgarian socialist economy already had on the people's mental health?"

"One direct result of our socialist economy," she said, "is

the very good organization of our public health services. The main emphasis in our health work is preventive medicine, and recently we have started the periodic check-up of the entire population, either where they work or in their homes, without waiting for them to get sick and go to a doctor.

"The early diagnosis of both physical and mental illness," she added, "and the creating of an environment where such illnesses cannot take root, are important contributions of socialism to mental heath."

She looked at her watch. It was time for her to leave. I asked just one more brief question: "How much does a patient pay, and how is the psychiatrist paid, for treatment which is sometimes continued over a very long period?"

"Pay? The patient doesn't pay anything. The psychiatrist, like all other physicians, receives his salary from the Government."

I then said that since this was a house visit, and quite beyond the normal call of duty—and since I was a foreigner and so made no contribution to their public-health fund—I'd like to know what I owed her for coming to examine me and prescribe for my sore throat.

"But nothing!" she exclaimed with a smile. "Doh vizhdane! (Good-bye!) Your sore throat will probably be better soon."

"Thank you very much," I said; "and—er—yes, I think it feels a little better already."

The door closed behind her. Guillermo sat there laughing. "You see!" he said. "It's our socialist system. You'll just have to get used to it."

CHAPTER 12

WITH RESPECT TO CREED
AND COLOR

CERTAIN INALIENABLE RIGHTS

Bulgaria's Constitution of 1947 guarantees to all her citizens equality before the law; it recognizes no privilege based on sex, national origin, color, creed, or property status. Advocacy of racial, national, or religious hatred is punishable by law. Citizens are guaranteed extensive personal rights and liberties, including freedom of conscience and of religion. The Church is separated from the State. The national minorities are granted the right to be taught in their own language.

Of the total 8 million population, about 7 million are of Bulgarian stock; some 700,000 are of Turkish origin; and 214,000 are Gypsies. There are also 21,000 Armenians, 10,000 Russians, 7,700 Greeks and 6,500 Jews.

Between 1878 and 1944 those Turks who remained in Bulgaria were treated as second-class citizens. Only a few of them attended school. Now practically all do. They have their own schools, taught in Turkish. In these, as in the schools of all the minority groups, the study of the Bulgarian language is obligatory. As we have seen, thirteen members of the National Assembly are of Turkish origin.

The status of the Gypsies is of special interest, partly because they too were second-class citizens before the war and most of them were very poor; also because Gypsies have been for centuries rootless and non-conformist, have taken no part in government, and have not been absorbed by "civilization." They have had little or no formal education. They were looked down on and discriminated against; they could not expect to mix with other people even if they wanted to. They used to move about the country with their few meager possessions in little horse-drawn covered carts, getting a few odd jobs, especially in spring and at harvest time, mainly repairing cooking pots and doing other minor work with metals. How do they fare now, in Bulgaria's socialist society?

Education and technical training are available free to Gypsies as to everyone else. Already some of them are physicians, lawyers, teachers, and—following a special talent of their people—musicians. Many of them work on cooperative farms and in factories. There is no discrimination against them. It used to be practically unheard of that a Gypsy married a Bulgarian, but now it is not uncommon. In economic, political, and social life, to be a Gypsy is no longer an obstacle.

A Bulgarian friend of mine who knows many Gypsies personally told me that in one village the first three private cars bought were bought by Gypsy families. They tend to have large families; in each of these families a number of working members chipped in and bought the car. Perhaps they had a nostalgia for their little carts and the open road!

A Bulgarian writer, after visiting a former Gypsy slum district on the outskirts of Sofia now transformed into a new housing project where many of the former inhabitants are relocated, comments, "It is really amazing how an age-long indifference to dirt and untidiness has been done away with in a single decade. It is the liquidation of poverty that has put an end to the bad habits." Not only that; he pays tribute also to "the immense work done by Bulgarian doctors, teachers, and public-health workers in bringing the principles of hygiene and political enlightenment to the Gypsy population."

WHAT HAPPENED TO THE JEWS

I had heard that the fate of the Jews in Bulgaria during the war was very different from that of Jews in Poland and other countries; so I sought an interview with someone who knew about it in detail. My wife and I spent a good part of a morning around a table with four leaders of the Cultural and Social Organization of Jews in Bulgaria, at their headquarters on Stamboliiski Boulevard, Sofia. They were Dr. Jossif Astrukov, their President, a tall distinguished-looking man and a colonel in the Bulgarian Army; Israel Mayer, Editor-in-Chief of their bi-weekly newspaper, *Jewish News* (he acted as spokesman and interpreter at our meeting since he spoke French); Avram Kalo, the Secretary; and Matei Julsari, Administrative Secretary. They received us with cordiality, and we had a most interesting talk together.

The friendship between the Bulgarians and the Jews, they told us, has existed for centuries. Both suffered under the Turkish yoke, and they fought side by side for liberation from the Turks. There were never any ghettoes in Bulgaria, nor did anti-Semitism exist among the people.

During World War II the Nazis in Sofia, and leaders of the Bulgarian Government who were collaborating with them, planned a deportation of Jews for March, 1943. When this plan became known, the Bulgarian Writers' Union, some bishops of the Bulgarian Orthodox Church, doctors, lawyers, workers, and village people protested vigorously and publicly.

"The Resistance forces of the Communist Party in Bulgaria were very strong," said Dr. Astrukov. "The Party told the people, 'We must not let the Jews be deported. If we allowed them to be deported, it would be a national disgrace.' Then, too, the Bulgarian Jews were taking part en masse in the struggle against fascism; in Bulgaria it was a common struggle—Bulgarians and Jews together."

Dr. Astrukov himself had been the leader of a Partisan detachment. Mr. Mayer had also been with the Partisans. Some hundreds of Jews were killed in this struggle.

After the war, there was found in the archives of the German Gestapo a report written by the German ambassador in Bulgaria in 1943. It was addressed to Nazi Foreign Minister von Ribbentrop. "The Jewish question in Bulgaria," it states, "is a little different from that in other countries. The Bulgarian people are not yet convinced that it is necessary to suppress the Jews or to send them to crematoriums."

In early 1943 a delegation composed of Bulgarians and Jews went to see the Vice-President of the National Assembly, a man named Dimiter Peshev. They urged him to do everything in his power to prevent the deportation of the Jews. He undertook to do so, and obtained the signatures of forty-three members of the National Assembly on a letter to the Prime Minister, demanding that the deportation order be rescinded. For this he was dismissed from the Parliament. But the King and the Government, even though allied with Nazi Germany, gave way under the pressure of public opinion. They didn't cancel the deportation order, but they postponed it until "a more appropriate time."

The "more appropriate time" never came. In September, 1944, the Soviet Army swept down swiftly, and the Government leaders were arrested. After the war, they were brought to trial. Some of them who had collaborated with the Nazis were condemned to death and executed. But Peshev was spared.

Those Parliament members who were ready to send the Jews to their death would also have liked to send Bulgarian and Jewish soldiers to fight against the Russians on the Eastern front. They were never able to do so. "Bulgarians and Jews," commented Mr. Mayer, "would not have fired on their Russian brothers."

Mr. M. S. Arnoni, editor of *The Minority of One* (published in Passaic, N. J.) and himself a survivor of the Litzmannstadt Ghetto in Lodz, Poland, and of the Auschwitz extermination camp, comments in his April, 1964, issue:

We were guarded by the hostility of the "Christians" surrounding the Ghetto much more effectively than by any physical fence. Where and why would you escape if there was a virtual certainty that the first "Christian" you encountered on the outside would give you away to the Germans? One of the appalling truths about the behavior of vast masses of people in countries such as Poland, Lithuania, Hungary, and Rumania during the war was the degree to which they

voluntarily cooperated with the Nazis in hunting down and extermi-
nating the Jews, even while themselves oppressed by the Germans.

In Bulgaria, the attitude and struggle of both Bulgarians and
Jews stand in honorable contrast to such collaboration.

There were about 50,000 Jews in Bulgaria before the war, of
whom 23,000 were living in Sofia; at present there are 6,500, of
whom 3,500 live in Sofia. What happened to the rest of them?

Right after the war, when the Germans had left and the
leaders of the old government had been driven out of office and a
new government was being organized, the Jews asked each
other, "What now? Is it going to be the same as before?" After
generations of unhappy experience with governments, they had at
first no confidence in any government.

Then, too, for them as for everyone else in the country, life
was very difficult at the end of the war. Many of their homes had
been destroyed, the whole economy was disrupted, and they
were left with practically nothing. It was at this point that the
Zionists came and offered them free passage to Israel and the
chance to begin life anew.

At the head of the Government in 1945 was Georgi Dimitrov.
He said: "Those who want to leave the country are free to do so.
And those who want to stay are likewise free to do so."

In that same year, when the Israeli-Arab war began, some 750
young Jews left Bulgaria secretly, via Cyprus, for Israel. Some
were killed in the fighting, others wounded. Practically all the
young men who survived remained in Israel, and a good many
of their friends and relatives in Bulgaria decided to join them
there. Thus, for a variety of reasons there was a large-scale
emigration of Bulgarian Jews—all of them to Israel.

Those who emigrated were mainly workers, artisans, and shopkeepers. They still speak Bulgarian. "If one goes to the districts
where they live," said Dr. Astrukov, "one might almost think
he were back in Bulgaria. They publish newspapers in Bulgarian;
they show Bulgarian films in their theaters; their way of cooking
remains Bulgarian."

When Bulgarian actors, musicians, dancers, and singers go to perform in Israel, they are received with special enthusiasm—in fact, with some nostalgia—by the Jews from Bulgaria.

Many Bulgarian Jews who are now citizens of Israel come back as tourists. And there is a considerable flow of visitors in both directions. By airplane it takes only three hours from Sofia to Tel Aviv; by boat (from Varna to Istanbul to Tel Aviv), three days. Many prefer to go by boat because they like to take a lot of typically Bulgarian presents—especially cheeses—to their relatives and friends, and if they went by plane they couldn't possibly get everything within the forty-four-pound luggage allowance.

Most of the Jews in Bulgaria live and work in the cities. Some of them have jobs in Government administration. Mr. Mayer, for example, has been for ten years in an administrative post; Mr. Kalo, the Secretary, works in the State Planning Office; the President, Dr. Astrukov, as has been said, is a colonel in the Bulgarian Army. Some are scientists, engineers, factory managers, economists, accountants, journalists, theatrical producers, artists, and movie actors. The majority are industrial workers and artisans.

Those who wish to become rabbis study abroad, either at their own expense or on scholarships. There is no school in Bulgaria for training rabbis, because of the limited need. There are synagogues in Sofia, Plovdiv, Stara Zagora and, in fact, all the larger cities.

I asked about the work of their Cultural and Social Organization. They organize lectures and discussions, I was told, and have various other cultural activities. "Many Jews who were in the Resistance," said Mr. Mayer, "and so couldn't finish their education are now enabled to do so, thanks to the supplementary financial aid from our organization. Tuition is free, but we help with the students' living expenses. Almost every Bulgarian Jewish family," he added with pride, "now has a child studying at the university. No distinction is made between Jews and other Bulgarian citizens; and the same is true, of course, regarding the Turkish, Armenian, and other minority groups."

CHURCH AND STATE

In some respects, religious groups in Bulgaria have more freedom today than before the present Government came to power. If the Church is not allowed to interfere in State affairs, the State, for its part, guarantees that it will not interfere in religious matters. The Constitution of 1947 declares the separation of Church and State, and recognizes the right of citizens to hold any religious belief, likewise the right to hold none.

For many years the Bulgarian Orthodox Church, within which are about 80 per cent of the religious people in the country, was under the tutelage of the State. In 1953 it was able to re-establish its ancient dignity as a patriarchate, which it had lost toward the end of the fourteenth century when the country was conquered by the Turks. Today it maintains relations with all Orthodox churches in the world and is a member of the World Council of Churches, which has its headquarters in Geneva. Patriarch Cyril is Vice-President of the Bulgarian National Peace Committee.

The second largest religious group, the Mohammedans, has some twelve hundred mosques in Bulgaria. In former times all Mohammedan religious institutions were controlled by the State; but now they have the right to appoint and dismiss their own priests and to spend their financial resources as they think best.

Catholics, Protestants, and Jews were discriminated against in the past, but not any more. The six denominations of Protestant churches have about twelve thousand members.

A law passed in 1949 provides that any denomination may open secondary and higher ecclesiastical schools by obtaining permission from the Government. The various religious groups raise funds from their land holdings and other property and from donations by their members. The State itself grants subsidies to the Bulgarian Orthodox Church, the Mohammedans, the Gregorian-Armenians, and the Jewish synagogues, in accordance with their needs. All the religious groups may publish literature of their own. The Synod of the Bulgarian Orthodox Church, for example, publishes a weekly church newspaper and a monthly magazine.

No such antagonism between Church and State as there is in some other countries has ever existed in Bulgaria. Throughout the centuries the Bulgarian Church has had its progressive aspect. Georgi Dimitrov has said, "We would not have had the new democratic Bulgaria of today, the Bulgaria of the Fatherland Front, if during the dark years of slavery our monasteries such as Rila had not existed, for they safeguarded the national pride and hopes of the Bulgarians, enabling them to survive as a nation."

The Government has set up a Committee on the Question of the Orthodox Church and Religious Cults. I had a talk with Mr. Dimiter Todorov, Chief of its Department for the Bulgarian Orthodox Church. "The way the religious organizations run their internal affairs concerns them alone," he said. "But the Church is not a State within the State. There are certain relations between the Church and State, as established by the Constitution and by law. Our Committee serves as liaison between the Church and the State, regulating all the questions that exist between them.

"The various sects do not have representatives on this Committee; this is a Government committee. But the head of each religious group may put his questions and problems before our Committee, and we transmit them to the Government."

Mr. Todorov said that neither the Government itself nor this Committee as its organ may make decisions on internal or religious matters. But questions arise which are of an economic and social character. The Church owns certain lands and buildings, and since land use now follows an over-all State plan, sometimes some of these Church lands are to be incorporated in a planned use. In such cases other, equivalent, land is given in exchange. Sometimes the Church is not satisfied; then the Committee acts as arbitrator.

The Church is not allowed to pursue goals which are contrary

to those of the State. No anti-State propaganda by the Church is
allowed. If some Church group has a complaint, the Committee
considers its point of view. Or if, for example, a priest comes
before the Committee and complains that some citizen has
prevented the celebration of the Mass, the Committee sees to it
that that person is punished.

"On the Committee," added Mr. Todorov, "we have nonbelievers. But they are friends of the Church, even though not in
ideology, and for this reason: the Church represents a part of our
people who are believers and who, at the same time, are helping
to build socialism in our country. These believers are loyal to
the State.

"In the West, some people misrepresent the relation between
our State and the Church. But in reality those relations are
friendly, showing that peaceful coexistence is possible, not only
between one State and another, but between the State and the
Church."

The New York *Times* of May 4, 1964, carried a front-page
story headed: "Bulgarians Riot at Sofia Church: Hundreds Reported in Clash with Police After Ban on Easter Midnight Mass."
To read only so far, the headline-skimmer might think: "So the
Government is cracking down on religion over there." But if you
read the article itself, you see first of all that the reporter was
not on the spot, not in Sofia, not even in Bulgaria—he was in
Belgrade. And he writes: "Hundreds of Bulgarian Christians
were reliably reported [by whom?] to have rioted early today
when armed policemen prevented them from attending a midnight Mass in the cathedral in Sofia in observance of Orthodox
Easter. Reports from Communist Bulgaria's capital said clashes
between the Orthodox faithful and the police had occurred in
front of Alexander Nevsky Church." But halfway through the
article you read that "when the crowds arrived for the Mass they
found the entrances blocked by youths shouting atheistic slogans.
The police intervened, according to the report, and closed the
doors 'to prevent incidents.' [These quotation marks are the
Times's.] It was then that the clashes occurred."

I wrote to a friend in Sofia and asked: "What are the facts

about that riot which the New York *Times* says you people had at the Alexander Nevsky Church on May 3?" The reply came back. "The New York *Times* or any Western paper *would* make a story out of an insignificant incident. The Government is not interfering with or banning church services; but some youths —there has been a trend toward atheistic or rather materialistic education in the various youth organizations—did make some trouble at the services last Easter. This year the militia was asked to watch so that no such incidents would occur; hence the presence of militia around the church. When a group of young people appeared and wanted to shout their atheistic slogans, the militia stopped them and protected the churchgoers from being bothered. It was a very minor incident; nobody paid any attention to it but those who wanted to make capital out of it."

Many people in Western countries look down their noses at the "godlessness" of the socialist countries. Such an attitude, it seems to me, comes with little grace from "Christians" who slaughtered each other by the millions in two world wars and are now preparing the third and final war.

Is it not strange that in many of the "Christian" countries the moral teachings of Christ have been brushed aside, and that many of these teachings flourish in actual fact today in a society led by nonbelievers? As an Irishman once said: "If we were all atheists, we might be able to live together like Christians."

BLACK AND FREE

There are many African students in Sofia attending the university and technical schools. Before I left home I had read an article in *Newsweek* (February 25, 1963) headed "Segregation in Sofia," in which it was stated that some Ghanian students found that "Bulgarians refused to sit beside Africans in buses or restaurants," and that Africans had to wait up to two hours to be served in restaurants in Sofia. Such articles may serve to distract attention from the attitude of many white Americans toward Negroes in the South (and not in the South alone), but

I can only report what I personally experienced plus information that I believe to be reliable.

It is true that some people, black or white, are not always courteous or understanding; incidents have taken place in Bulgaria from both sides. But by and large, the African students are being well received there. Sometimes friction results from a genuine misunderstanding. Here is an instance of it:

A Bulgarian acquaintance told me that one day when he was in a trolley bus he saw a Negro student start to enter by the front door. The driver motioned to him to get in at the rear door. Not this young man! He grew angry with the driver, called him a "racist," and said that there were some countries where he would be made to sit in the rear of the bus, but he had thought this wouldn't happen in Bulgaria.

What were the facts? In Bulgaria everybody is required to enter the bus by the rear door, because that's where the conductor is. He, or often she, sits at a little booth near the door, and that's where you pay your fare.

As for discrimination in restaurants, my wife and I had occasion to dine in some of the best in Sofia, and Negroes were often there. So far as we could see, they were served and treated just like anyone else. One evening we were having dinner at the Restaurant Berlin, across the square from the above-mentioned Alexander Nevsky Church. An African student, when he had finished his meal at a nearby table, came over and greeted us in English. We invited him to sit down. He was from Sudan, he told us, and was studying dentistry. He had been in Bulgaria for two years. We asked him what had led to his choice of Bulgaria.

"The Sudan Government," he answered, "though now independent, requires that all postgraduate studies be carried on in England. This is because the top Government people in Sudan had their training in England and they think it is the best place for such studies. However, I was to do not postgraduate work, but college-level work, so I was free to go elsewhere.

"All the socialist countries," he continued, "are offering scholarships to African students. Bulgaria offers each year thirty scholarships for Sudanese in various fields of unspecified studies. A committee in Sudan gives each qualified student his choice among three countries—for example, Switzerland, Czechoslovakia, and Pakistan. I wanted to know a Slavic language, and was given the choice between Yugoslavia, Poland, and Bulgaria."

Friends of his, he said, who had studied in Bulgaria and had returned home to Sudan for their vacation, had told him that the Bulgarian people by tradition are hospitable; that the food in Bulgaria is somewhat like that in Sudan; and that the academic standards are good. He gave still another reason that helped him to make a decision. "Bulgaria," he said, "was for long under the Turks; Sudan also was invaded and ruled by the Turks, before the British came." Thus he felt in advance a kinship with the Bulgarians because, as he put it, they and his people had "suffered under the same misrule."

When he had arrived in Bulgaria two years before, he didn't know a word of the language. It took him the first year to acquire a working knowledge of it, including the special terminology for dentistry.

He commented that learning the language was opening up to him not only the study of dentistry but also "the language and literature of some 200,000,000 people—of Bulgaria, the Soviet Union, and Yugoslavia at least." I asked him if he would be assured of a job when he returned home. He smiled and said: "We have a population of 13,000,000 in Sudan—and there are fifteen dentists."

One day I was in a bookshop in Sofia looking for a copy of the little statistical yearbook, but none of the clerks (and this is unusual) spoke English, French, or German. Seeing two African students there, I asked them in French if they could help me. They were from Guinea, had been in Bulgaria for four years, and spoke Bulgarian fluently. They bridged the language gap for me very agreeably.

At the big hotel where we were staying in Sofia, I met a young Negro medical student. He and I were sitting waiting to get our hair cut by the hotel barber. He told me in French that he was one of eleven students in Bulgaria from Cameroons. They were studying to be doctors, architects, and engineers.

These are small incidents; not much happened but a few pleasant words together. Yet I could not help thinking that in the capital of my own country Negroes were not dining in the best restaurants, frequenting the bookshops, or getting their hair cut in the big hotels.

CHAPTER 13

A BIT ABOUT INDUSTRY

The Director of the Vassil Kolarov Electric Power Equipment Plant was understandably proud of the plant's achievements. As I sat in his office in the administration building, he waved his hand in the direction of the large machine shops we could see out the window, and said: "In 1950 this place was an open field. Today we are producing—and exporting—heavy-duty electric motors, power transformers, high-voltage equipment, and generators for small hydroelectric plants. We export seventy per cent of our motors. They are being used today in more than twenty-four countries—in Europe, Cuba, Asia, and Africa."

Some five thousand people, most of whom had never been inside a factory until a few years ago, are producing this equipment. One third of them are women.

The Director told me that at the start the plant received the help of specialists from the Soviet Union and other socialist countries. Bulgarian engineers and technicians, through such help and by going to study in those countries, acquired training in machine design as well as in production. "The motors and much other equipment which we are making now," said the Director, "were designed by Bulgarians. From time to time our engineers go to other socialist countries to acquire the latest technical information. Then they come back and train our workers to produce equipment of high quality and of the most modern design."

Among the socialist countries there is a Council for Mutual Economic Assistance—a clearing house for information on design and production and on each country's needs and manufacturing capabilities. In accordance with decisions of this Council, the various socialist countries specialize in certain products which they manufacture both for themselves and for the other countries.

A trade-union official from the plant, who was with us at the interview, told me that about 98 per cent of the workers are members of the union; the other 2 per cent are mainly newcomers. "Practically everyone in the plant," he said, "works to increase production, to fulfill the Plan, and thus to better his own and the people's lives—and works also for peace and socialism."

Some of the workers are considered to be "pioneers in building the society of the future," he added. "This is because of their exemplary work and attitude. They have got rid of old ways of life, old attitudes, not only in the plant but also in their family life. They look for ways to help others."

The plant has its own crèches and kindergartens. And on weekends, workers can go to its holiday house on Mount Vitosha, which takes three hundred and fifty people at a time, and they stay there free of charge. The plant also has another holiday house at the seashore near Varna.

After about an hour's interview, the Director left me with the trade-union man, who was to show me around the plant. I was invited to join him after that in the big hall at a folk-song and folk-dance program which members of the plant were putting on in celebration of International Women's Day (March 8).

As we walked through the big buildings past rows of punch presses and lathes, we came to a group of women who were assembling electric motors. Most of these women, my guide said, had come not long ago from villages. They had placed some pots of flowers and trained some vines near their benches; and at the rear, on the wall, they had put a large portrait of a man whom I didn't recognize as any of the Bulgarian leaders. My guide told me that this was a portrait of the Greek anti-fascist journalist Manolis Glezos.

"Why have the women put his picture there?" I asked.

He explained that during World War II, when Greece was occupied by the Germans, a young Greek named Manolis Glezos climbed up the Acropolis with a few of his comrades, pulled down the Nazi flag, and raised the Greek flag in its place. He was arrested and put in prison. After the war he was set free and became very active in Greek political life; but a reactionary government was imposed on Greece, and he was put in prison again, there to remain for a long time. Only two or three years ago he was set free, by a new and more liberal government. This was partly the result of a vigorous campaign on his behalf by progressive journalists and others in many countries.

These women workers had put up a sign near the portrait. It said: "We women consider you to be a member of our production team. We work better because of knowing of your courage and unflinching spirit."

* * *

At the Kremikovtsi Industrial Complex, half an hour's drive from Sofia, everything is "the biggest." Huge chimney smoke-stacks, blast furnaces, acres of machinery in long, low buildings; a maze of power lines; between buildings, all sorts and sizes of overhead pipes—estimated to equal in length the distance from Sofia to Varna (three hundred miles). Trucks, noise, soft-coal smoke, huge overhead cranes rolling along in the upper regions of workshops. Railroad marshaling yards bigger than those at Sofia station. Was this the Soviet Union, the United States, China—or little Bulgaria?

A young engineer took me and my interpreter around. It was a dizzying environment. Man is an animal; how can he feel at home here? But, if it is necessary . . . The interpreter commented: "Even the engineers are puzzled by all this." By this he meant, probably, that it was much too complicated for him to understand and he knew it was for me, too. Bulgarian poets have found themselves at a loss to describe it; some of them even used the word "beautiful." In any case, it is considered a necessary step on the way to the future.

For some years now, women as well as men, from every part of the country, have toiled on the concrete and brick labyrinth, even in freezing weather, to help bring this industrial giant into being. Numbing wind swept through this broad valley, which in the winter of 1962–63, lay under three feet of snow. The wind beat against the rising smokestacks and walls, against the quilted coats of the men and women, many of whom had arrived fresh from the countryside. It tried to tear off their caps with the brown plush earflaps tied down; it howled "No!" to man's astounding boldness. But the young hearts beating under the quilted coats, the confident and quiet minds under those snug caps, said "Yes!" And the yesses have it.

In one of the buildings where iron is smelted, an overhead traveling crane came rolling down the hall. Up in its control cab a young woman with a blue kerchief tied around her head peered intently through one of its windows. She pulled a lever. A cable unrolled and let down a five-hundred-pound hook— itself enough to knock a man down and crush him. She lowered the hook into the murky depths where awesome leviathans sputtered and glowed. Flames were spurting out of cracks in the oven where iron ore was being reduced to liquid. A couple of men on the floor eased the hook under the bail of a bucket full of scrap iron, and away soared hook and bucket to the far end of the hall.

Some of those who are building socialism and moving on toward the next stage of their grand Plan, the building of communism, apparently have to live for a while in this purgatory, this trial by fire, on the unexplored way toward an earthly paradise. Among these machines, and among these men and women, I again asked myself the question: Will man know how to—and will he be wise enough to—keep tight control over the machines he has conjured up?

The young engineer, Alexander Zlatarski, who showed us around, had graduated from the Institute of Chemistry and Technology in Sofia in 1963. He now left us, in a shed that housed a technical library used by engineers and technicians, and went to find an older engineer who could answer the questions which he assumed I would ask. But my questions were not that advanced—or rather, they were philosophical, not technical; and of whom could I ask them here, except of myself?

The door opened and in came Zlatarski's older colleague—a slender young woman, Katia Sankeva. She told me she had graduated from engineering school back in 1959. She pulled out of her overcoat pocket two big notebooks full of facts and statistics, prepared to offer me twenty times more of them than I could understand or use.

Bulgaria, she told me, in building its heavy-industry base, needs of course a great quantity of iron and steel. According to the Plan, the Kremikovtsi Industrial Complex, when completed, is to produce about three million tons of pig iron, three and a half million tons of steel, and three million tons of rolled stock each year. Some sixteen thousand people are to be working there. Meanwhile, big housing projects for the workers are going up between the plant and the Vienna-Istanbul highway, which passes nearby.

Engineer Katia Sankeva's special field is the production of nonferrous metals. She had had a five-year course in general metallurgy, plus one year in this special field. She had been one of eighty students in ferrous and nonferrous metals; about half of them were women.

She and her husband, who is also a metallurgical engineer, have a two-year-old son. I asked her if she would want her son to follow in her profession. She looked at me jotting down notes in my notebook and said with a little smile: "Perhaps it will be better for him to have some easier job—say, that of a writer."

* * *

In November, 1963, George Meany, President of the AFL-CIO, said in New York to a convention of that 13,500,000-member organization:

[Automation] is rapidly becoming a real curse to this society. . . . Every big corporation in America is in a mad race to produce more and more with less and less labor, without any feeling as to what it may mean to the whole national economy. . . . Serious-minded scientists and public officials who are knowledgeable on this subject see jobs being eliminated at the rate of tens of thousands a month. Competent technologists in this field think of the day a few years hence when all the production we need will be furnished by less than 25 per cent of the manpower we have. . . . We cannot take the position that this system [of government] is invulnerable, that it cannot collapse. This system can go down the drain on this very one problem . . . unless our business community, our great captains of industry and our politicians wake up to this problem.

In March, 1964, the Ad Hoc Committee on the Triple Revolution sent to President Lyndon Johnson and Congressional leaders a statement on three closely related revolutions: in cybernation ("brought about by the combination of the computer and the automated self-regulating machine"), weaponry, and human rights. Its thirty-two signers include economists, labor leaders, historians, and publishers. (Among them are W. H. Ferry, Michael Harrington, Ralph L. Helstein, H. Stuart Hughes, Stewart Meacham, A. J. Muste, Gunnal Myrdal, Linus Pauling, Gerard Piel, and Bayard Rustin.)

It made this surprising proposal: "Wealth produced by machines rather than by men is still wealth. We urge, therefore, that society, through its appropriate legal and governmental institutions, undertake an unqualified commitment to provide every individual and every family with an adequate income as a matter of right."

"That would be socialism!" some might cry. But no. As some American economists have recently pointed out, our private-enterprise system might conceivably provide such an income as a means of keeping the lid on and *preventing* socialism—that is, preventing a change to public ownership of the means of production. The Ad Hoc Committee's proposal, however, does foreshadow a problem of the automation age, a problem which presumably will be tackled in one way by a capitalist country and in another way by a socialist country.

Premier Todor Zhivkov of Bulgaria said, in 1961, to a national Conference of Rationalizers and Innovators: "We call on you, innovators and inventors, engineers, designers and scientists, to give your creative thought full play, to design better machines, tools and apparatus, to work persistently to improve their quality, to work for the adoption of assembly-line production, and wherever possible, automation."

During an interview in Sofia with the Secretary of the Central Council of the Bulgarian Trade Unions, Mr. Grigor Iliev, I asked him what the trade unions' attitude was toward automation. "Our trade unions," he replied, "are working for more and more technical progress in the factories. We are very much for automation and mechanization. These automatic installations free workers to go to other jobs which are waiting for them and where they are greatly needed."

Even aside from the ever-present danger of nuclear war, there are some grave problems related to industrialism which, it seems to me, the people of both East and West are tending to brush aside or minimize. Here are several of them:

The rapid population growth throughout most of the world.
The rapid depletion of non-renewable natural resources.
The grave disadvantages that scientific progress brings to man along with its advantages.
The physically softening situation in which the human animal finds himself when he is drawn out of his rural habitat and destined, apparently, to live in a brick, concrete, and asphalt environment for most of the remaining days of his life.

Then, too, there is the assumption, in East and West alike, that technological progress will, of itself, somehow lead to the enrichment of human lives; and that the more *things* we have, the better—apparently forever. This is not only "communist" or "capitalist" thinking; it is a part of a worldwide assumption and, it seems to me, is unsound for the long run. I have found people in Poland, Yugoslavia, and Bulgaria, and at home in the United States, who have ready answers to these questions; sometimes too ready, too much by the book. I have also talked with a few people who are deeply concerned about them. The more industrialized a nation becomes, the more its people will,

I think, have to re-examine their actual environment and their goals. Will it then be too late?

In socialist countries there is a cheerful assumption that under socialism—with a lot of hard and heroic work, of course—everything will turn out all right. That after another decade or two or three—barring a world war—the main problems will have been solved. That the population curve will level off satisfactorily (people moving into cities will have better education, fewer and healthier children, etc.). That man will master science and nature, and will somehow keep healthy in an urban and industrial environment.

I wish I could be convinced of this. The Bulgarians and the other socialist peoples have struggled and worked so long and so hard for their decent world! They may be able to solve *some* major problems—full employment with automation, for example—but what about certain others, such as population and natural resources? For no one country or group of countries can solve these problems alone. Inevitably, in the long run, any country will be vitally affected by what happens in the rest of the world.

But on the more constructive side: many problems facing man in an industrial environment are *common to both West and East.* And as such they could be a common bond between us. Are we not capable of putting an end to the stupid and short-sighted Cold War, and sitting down together to see if we can reach some basic, planet-wide solutions?

CHAPTER 14

THE BIG FARMS

2,000 YEARS WITH THE SAME PLOW

In the Archaeological Museum in Plovdiv, I saw a metal plow-point made by a Thracian about two thousand years ago. Flattish on top, with a wide-angle point, it is in shape rather like an Indian arrowhead. With it the ancient farmer could have disturbed the earth to a depth of about three inches.

In the Ethnographic Museum in Sofia are an iron plowpoint and the wooden plow on which it fits, of a kind generally used until after 1944. There is not much difference between these two plows.

On the eve of 1944 Bulgarian agriculture was among the most backward in all Europe. Aside from the larger holdings of landlords, there were about a million individual farms, cut up into twelve million strips of land, averaging an acre or less per strip. The peasants tilled them with wooden, iron-tipped plows drawn by cattle. There were in the whole country some 516,000 such plows. Other farm implements throughout Bulgaria were, as in Biblical times, the scythe, the sickle, the hoe, and a primitive threshing device. For transport, both of farm produce and of farmers: 316,000 wooden carts—198,000 with iron rims on their wooden wheels.

Irrigation? Donkeys used to plod around in a circle, turning wheels that lifted a little water out of a river—for those peasants who lived at the edge of a suitable river—to keep the crops from drying up.

The peasants had other problems, too. They were exploited by the landlords, by the dealers who bought their produce, by the city merchants who set prices, and by heavy taxes. A large proportion of them sank under these burdens, lost whatever little land they had, and in the hope of keeping from starving, hired out as farm hands. Where to look for help? To the Church, perhaps, or to the State? The peasants had a saying that "God is too high and the king is too far."

A COOPERATIVE GIANT

Shortly before the end of the nineteenth century, peasants began forming consumer cooperatives and credit unions for their protection. The landlords and money-lenders took a dim view of these innovations, of course. These early co-ops were small. Twenty regional and national cooperative organizations developed—and quarreled with each other. But in 1947 they were all brought together in a Central Cooperative Union. Now there are the cooperative farms; producers' cooperatives in the towns (tailors, shoemakers, etc.); and consumer co-ops in both towns and villages.

In the period between the two world wars, many peasants pooled their lands to form cooperative farms. Thus there was some precedent which helped to increase the number of such farms rapidly after 1944.

The Land Reform law of 1946 expropriated arable holdings of more than fifty acres (seventy-five acres in the Dobroudja region). Part of this expropriated land was distributed to poor peasants and to cooperative farms; part became State property and was used for the new State farms (of which more later).

By 1957 there were 3,200 cooperative farms; these have been gradually consolidated, on the initiative of the farmers themselves. By the end of 1964 there were just under 1,000 of them —but all much bigger, of course, than before: their average size is about 11,000 acres. They are among the largest in the world, and include about 98 per cent of Bulgaria's arable land.

On a hot August day I visited such a farm, half an hour's drive from Sofia. It has 14,000 acres of arable land. It lies in a flat valley and extends to low mountains in the far distance on either side. Five villages and one town are included within this farm. It produces wheat, corn, cattle, sheep, sunflower seed (for cooking oil), and vegetables; also tree fruits and other fruits (for example, it has 60 acres in strawberries and the same in raspberries).

As the sunburnt young chairman of the farm and my interpreter and I got out of the car and approached a cornfield, we met a cheerful elderly peasant with a walrus mustache, who had a shotgun slung over his shoulder. The chairman greeted him in friendly fashion, took the shotgun, looked through both barrels and saw that it was not loaded. He handed it back to the guard with a smile.

"Two people can be scared by this gun," he remarked, "he who sees it and he who holds it. But," he added, "this comrade helps to keep the sheep out of the cornfields."

It was in 1950 that this cooperative farm was started, but for the first few years some of the farmers were not convinced that it was more profitable to work the land with machines than in the age-old way.

I asked if it was unusual to have so many as five villages and a town within one cooperative farm. "No," replied the chairman; "the farm next to ours now takes in eleven villages."

More than twelve thousand acres of the farm are already irrigated, from the large artificial lake formed by a dam on the Isker River, some miles away. (The lake also provides hydroelectric power and a recreation area.) The chairman of the farm seemed not at all concerned about the long August drought.

Today 18 per cent of Bulgaria's arable land is irrigated, a figure which places her already among the leading countries in the world in this respect. But her goal for 1980 is much higher: 50 per cent.

I was surprised to learn that only 18 per cent of the total working population of the farm I was visiting are now employed there. (In the whole country, however, about 50 per cent of the working population are still in agriculture.) Most of the others have jobs in nearby industries. They earn more in the factories; there is a big drive on to establish the country's heavy industries; and the increasing use of large-scale farm machinery has freed many people for other work.

The "manpower" here is largely womanpower. In contrast to the prolonged and often lonely drudgery of farm work in the old days, the women work an eight-hour day, in teams of ten to fifteen members. Later, we drove over to the ensilage pits where, between masonry walls, women with pitchforks were distributing the fodder as it was dumped from the tractor-pulled wagons. It was clear from their joking among themselves and with the chairman that teamwork had very real social advantages for them.

The farm is divided into sections based on the village areas, and each section has an agricultural scientist and a specialist in animal husbandry. Over all there is a chief agricultural scientist and a chief of animal husbandry; these two are among the members of the farm's executive committee. The general meeting of the farm members elects the chairman and the executive committee, and can replace them at any time.

Each village has a kindergarten where mothers can leave their small children during the work day. More than half the cost of a child's maintenance there is borne by the farm—all of it if both parents work on the farm.

While we were talking at the edge of the cornfield, two tractors came toward us, side by side. One was pulling a combine harvester that cut the corn, chopped it up, and poured it through a long pipe into the wagon, which was pulled by the other tractor. Several bronzed, kerchiefed women were distributing the fodder—"Wisconsin maize," the chairman called it—on top of the load.

These machines, made in the Soviet Union, had been rented from a Machine and Tractor Station until the previous year; then the farm committee decided it would be better economy to buy them. Many other prosperous farms are doing the same.

On a cooperative farm, a member's earnings depend on the amount of work he has done in a certain period, and on the farm's over-all production. There are general bonuses at the end of the fiscal year, and some bonuses to individuals who have done exceptionally good work. If a member wants to withdraw from the farm, he may do so and is then given a piece of land of equal value to his, on the edge of the big farm. But this rarely happens, since it is now plain to almost everybody that with modern machine cultivation one can make a better living on a cooperative farm.

The eighty-five State farms, which average even a little larger than the cooperative farms, are differently organized. They are Government-owned, and the workers are paid fixed wages just as in a factory. Usually a State farm is set up for some special research—for example, the development of new varieties of wheat or grapes. It studies scientific problems of agriculture; tests and demonstrates new methods of large-scale farm management; provides raw materials for industry; and supplies high-grade seed, seedlings, cattle, fruit trees, etc., to the cooperative farms.

Each farmer, whether on a cooperative or a State farm, has, if he wishes, a small plot of about half an acre to cultivate after his normal hours of work on the big farm and on weekends. He may own a cow, two sows, two goats, three to five sheep, etc. What he produces on his plot is free from taxes, and he may sell any of it without restriction.

While some farms, especially in hilly terrain, are not modernized, nevertheless "mechanization" is a favorite word with the Bulgarians now. On some of their chicken farms they have already installed apparatus which prepares and delivers the poultry feed, collects the eggs, and cleans the hen houses. One man is the button pusher: he says "Go!" to five thousand laying hens. And yet only a few years ago cooperative farmers were telling each other that poultry raising was unprofitable. Mechanization has also come to the lowly pig; with it, one man can take care of fifteen hundred pigs.

Bulgaria's climate is especially favorable for fruit growing: a cool spring, warm summer, mild autumn, and snowbound winter. She holds first place in the world for the quantity of fresh tomatoes exported, and second place in Europe for the export of dessert grapes. Most of the perishable vegetables and fruits are now flown out, by Bulgarian Air Lines ("TABSO"), to Austria, Germany, Sweden, Great Britain, and other countries.

Constant experimentation is going on. It has recently been decided to change from high- to low-growing fruit trees. These start bearing at an earlier age, bear more regularly, and give larger and better fruit. They are easier to prune, spray, and pick from, and are less liable to injury by winds. This change-over began on a large scale only in 1960. On trips through the country-side I have observed broad seas of these young fruit trees, on level land and up hillsides, extending as far as the eye could see.

Bulgarian apple growers are now concentrating on ten varieties, mainly those which are in demand abroad. Among them are Golden Permain, Borovinka, Delicious, Jonathan, and Berska Rose.

In the export of attar of roses—used in making perfumes, cosmetics, soaps, medicines, and food—Bulgaria is again first in the world. During Hitler's regime, her rose crop all but disappeared, because Nazi Germany was producing essential oils synthetically and put effective pressure on the Bulgarian government to pay a subsidy for every acre of rose fields taken out of cultivation. But since 1944, and especially since the cooperative farms grew strong, the rose fields have been rapidly restored. (What a beautiful sight is the Valley of Roses!)

The Thracians were the first in that part of the world to grow grapes. Homer says that the Thracian town of Piso sent ships laden with wine to the Greeks who were besieging Troy. Academician Nedelchev, aged seventy-four, is a pioneer in modern grape culture. The experimental field over which he presides has more than five hundred local and foreign varieties. He crossed the "Sultanka" with an Italian variety and obtained larger grapes and four times greater productivity. More than ten tons of grapes per acre have been achieved from the "Bolgar" variety.

I didn't see a harvest celebration but was told they are very

gay and colorful. Even before 1944, when the level of farm production would not have seemed conducive to celebrations, there
were dancing and singing, with attractive folk costumes and
customs. Some of this still remains, for when peasants become
members of cooperative farms, they transplant some of these
old customs there. Nowadays, instead of bringing an ornamental
harvest wreath to a landlord, they bring it to the chairman of the
cooperative farm. And, as for generations past, there is feasting,
singing, and dancing far into the night.

INSTEAD OF THE THORN

My wife and I sat down to Turkish coffee and cakes with
Engineer Marin Toshkov of the Committee on Forests and
Forest Industries. He told us that within the Committee a service
had been set up to preserve natural resources—forests, water,
soil, plants, animals, and fish. And voluntary local committees
have been formed in cities and villages, which make proposals
regarding local conservation needs. They may recommend that a
certain forest not be cut any more. Or they may propose that a
certain area be made a national park. The national Committee
in Sofia considers each proposal, and if it agrees, issues an order
declaring the proposal to be a "national goal." At present, six
areas have been declared national parks, among them Mount
Vitosha, the Pirin Mountains, and—on the seacoast—the Golden
Sands and Ropotamo River areas. Lumbering is not allowed in
these parks. They are for beauty, health, and recreation.

Bulgaria has also designated fifty-two areas as wild-life reser-
vations. Here everything is left in its natural state. They are
sanctuaries for animals, birds, and fish. There are footpaths for
the public, but no one is allowed to gather flowers, build fires, or
camp there.

There are sixty varieties of flowers that the public may not pick
anywhere in Bulgaria. Some of them are of medicinal value;
others are very rare, and there is danger that they might become

extinct. Some four hundred different animals and birds are likewise under the protection of the Committee.

The Committee has a tremendous program of tree planting, much of it done by volunteers on vacation. In two years alone, 1962 and 1963, as much territory was reforested as in the sixty years immediately preceding September, 1944.

Each spring, there is a National Forest Week, with lectures in the schools, and exhibits on forests, flowers, animals, and birds. Competitions are held in photography, painting, and writing concerned with forests and conservation.

Each school boy and girl (and many an adult too) spends about two days a year helping to renew the forests. The Committee on Forests also organizes camps in the woods during vacation time, and pays all expenses including transportation and food. Here young people work four or five hours a day, and have the rest of the time free. Getting to know the woods well, they come to regard them as their own, to be cherished and protected.

In the schools a much-prized card is given to each high-school boy or girl who shows evidence of the required maturity, discipline, and knowledge. It is issued by the Committee on Forests and Forest Industry, Council of Ministers, and is entitled "Official Card of a Defender of Nature." It carries a photograph of the owner. It states that he is "authorized to reprimand those who violate the laws on the preservation of nature, on forests, hunting, and fishing; to verify permits; to demand that violations be discontinued; and to become a witness in case the violators are liable to be fined." Before being accorded this honor, the boy or girl must have learned a good deal about the trees, flowers, and animals of the region.

As in many other countries, much of the once-rich natural forests of oak, beech, and other trees has been destroyed over the centuries, by cutting and by fires; and the earth has been laid open to erosion. It is a formidable task to build back a forest on slopes covered with little but fragments of rock, the topsoil having long ago blown away or washed down into the valley. But the time is not far off when the results of Bulgaria's afforestation program will provide a clear example for many other nations. Then, in the words of the prophet Isaiah: "The mountains and the hills shall break forth before you into singing, and all the trees of the field shall clap their hands. Instead of the thorn shall come up the fir tree, and instead of the brier shall come up the myrtle tree."

CHAPTER 15

THE ARTS IN SOCIALIST BULGARIA

Up to now, very little has been published in the United States about contemporary Bulgaria. But in Bulgaria the Foreign Languages Press (1 Levski Street, Sofia) has issued a number of publications in English—on Bulgarian history, the arts, archaeology, education, government, economics, public health, industry, agriculture, and so on; also some novels, short stories, and poetry. For example: A *Short History of Bulgaria* (illustrated, 462 pages, 1963); the novel *Under the Yoke*, by Ivan Vazov; and the monthly illustrated magazine *Bulgaria*, which has articles on many aspects of Bulgarian life. Balkantourist (Lenin Square, Sofia) publishes in various languages, including English, guide-books, maps and other material for tourists. Among recent books on Bulgaria published in England is A *History of Bulgaria, 1393–1885*, by Mercia MacDermott (George Allen & Unwin, London, illustrated, 354 pages, 1962).

While talking with a Bulgarian acquaintance, I happened to use the phrase "economic and cultural life." He commented that Bulgarians, in the present stage of their country's development, had "more cultural life than economic." And indeed, while Bulgarians are still comparatively poor in "the things of this world," they are rich in spirit, in ideals, in achievement. Bulgarian novelists, short-story writers, poets, playwrights, and directors are not pessimistic or frustrated. They do not write sensational stuff. Painters and sculptors, likewise, from what I saw in a number of exhibits in Sofia, do not consider that life is not worth living, nor a disappointment, nor a racket, nor a rat race. In short, Bulgarian life is vigorous and forward-looking.

The current literature and drama are often full of struggle

and may have a tragic ending, but the ending lifts you up, not lets you down. Although selfish, anti-social characters are also portrayed and may as in real life sometimes win out, the emphasis is on courage and, above all, on strength arising from and devoted to the people.

Many stories and films describe the struggle against the Turks, under the yoke, and against Bulgarian reactionaries in the period before World War II. Also the struggle against the Nazis who occupied the country; problems and successes in developing "the new man"; and the conflict in attitude between those whose interests are mainly selfish and those whose sympathies are social and humanistic. Bulgarian writing is a part of the nationwide effort to build socialism, and a favorite theme is how prejudice, mistrust, and alienation from society and from oneself are overcome.

It is forbidden to publish or to import pornographic literature. This is not a Communist ruling; it is a pre-1944 law which is still enforced. Newspapers and magazines do not print stories about the private lives of movie stars or anyone else. To do so would be considered in bad taste and an invasion of the rights of the individual.

American films are very expensive to import. The funds allocated for them and for other foreign films are used, as a Bulgarian friend put it, "for those that have artistic value and human relevance, not mere cheap entertainment."

At the opera one evening (it was *Tosca*, beautifully presented), I heard several English people during intermission agreeing that the Sofia opera was as fine, in acting, voices, costumes and scenery as that in Covent Garden. At present, the Sofia National Opera has a repertoire of thirty-four operas and eleven ballets. Opera and theater are not only nor mainly for the well-to-do; they are subsidized by the Government and are brought within the means of everybody. The best seat in the opera house in Sofia costs a little over a dollar; a seat in the back of the top gallery costs about the price of a cup of coffee.

This little country with about the population of Massachusetts and Connecticut together has five State opera companies, nine symphony orchestras, and many excellent theatrical companies, choirs, and dance groups. One reason for so much talent is the Bulgarians' deep-rooted musical tradition. Under the Turkish yoke, folk songs kept alive a sense of national unity and hope. People sang at farm work, at weddings, and on holidays in the public squares. And now there is widespread free musical education.

The most famous of all the folk ensembles is the State Folk Song and Dance Company, whose director is the composer Philip Koutev. They had just returned from a tour of the United States when we were in Sofia. We saw them three times—a feast for eye and ear. Since their first public appearance, in 1952, this ensemble has given concerts to enthusiastic audiences in Austria, Belgium, Canada, China, Czechoslovakia, France, Great Britain, Holland, Israel, Italy, Korea, Mongolia, Poland, Rumania, Syria, the United States, the U.S.S.R., Vietnam, and Yugoslavia.

Practically every factory and cooperative farm has a somewhat similar group, or one for instrumental music or dramatics. Each year the Ministry of Education and Culture, and the District People's Councils, hold local and national contests among such groups.

The Committee for Friendship and Cultural Relations with Foreign Countries (5 Ruski Boulevard, Sofia) was set up to help Bulgarian cultural organizations develop contacts abroad. It also maintains relations with foreign organizations concerned with friendship between their countries and Bulgaria. It organizes Bulgarian exhibitions, artistic and scientific, to be sent abroad; arranges for sending cultural and scientific workers to other countries; and receives foreign ones. It does not deal with any commercial activity.

At the rest home of the Union of Cultural Workers, in Borovets, I met one of Bulgaria's most distinguished actresses, People's Artist Zorka Yordanova. Since she has acted in many plays both before 1944 and after the big change-over, I asked her what differences she had noticed in production and acting, then and more recently, in the same play.

She replied that even though a play by Shakespeare, Goethe, or Schiller is produced with exactly the same words now as before 1944, the director can change the emphasis. An example is the role of the grave digger in *Hamlet*. Before the war, minor roles were often given to rather inexperienced actors; now, when what the minor character has to say is considered important, a better actor is assigned this role. Even in a major role, with the same words, one can give a different emphasis.

"The theater," she said, "is very popular in Bulgaria, and the plays give rise to much discussion by the people. Even in small towns there are theaters and dramatic groups."

She commented that Arthur Miller's *Death of a Salesman*, which was playing in Sofia at the time, was an absorbing human drama and greatly interested Bulgarian audiences.

Many other foreign plays, new and old, come to Bulgaria. Recently a classical Greek tragedy, presented in Sofia in Greek by a cast from Athens, was tremendously popular.

Contemporary Bulgarian motion pictures, like the literature and the stage plays, often carry a specific political message. Such a work is a new color film we saw in Sofia. It is the story of the thirteenth-century swineherd Ivailo, who led a present revolt against a tsar who was ineffective in opposing the Tartar invaders. The film has a cast of thousands, complete with helmets, spears, broadswords, and devices for scaling fortress walls. As a spectacular film it can satisfy the most action-minded. But aside from the medieval pageantry and battles there is a message. The director of the film states it as follows: "We have done our best to show that Ivailo's strength lies in his close ties with the people and his correct grasp of their aspirations."

After the tsar is killed, two of his boyars approach Ivailo, and "flattering words pour from their lips like fish out of a willow basket." They propose that he marry the tsar's widow—a haughty, seductive Grecian woman who would gladly hand Ivailo a goblet of poisoned wine—and that he reign as the new tsar in Turnovo. This, with some misgivings, he finally does.

The book *Ivailo,* on which the film was based, develops in detail the psychological struggle of the peasant leader. What will happen to his own trusted men among the luxuries of the court? Indeed, after a while "the new and easier life in Turnovo began to affect these simple souls." And he himself, having married a serpent of a queen, gradually felt corrupted. "Something had gone from his spirit, his soul had changed. Had he lost the vigor that had amazed the Tartars? Oh, how weak that vigor was against craftiness, against hypocrisy, against all the passions and vices which surrounded him like a wall, higher and stronger than the wall of a fortress!" And we have here at this layer of the story—after the battle scenes, after Ivailo's "close ties with the people and his correct grasp of their aspirations"—a subtler theme. It is a problem that confronts many governments and institutions, socialist as well as non-socialist, and it has never yet been satisfactorily solved: How to maintain honesty, simplicity, and decency after the crisis of struggle is over, and when living is easy. How to pass on the torch to the next generation.

While in Borovets, I had a talk with a director of documentary films, Mr. Numa Belogorski. He told me that although twenty years ago the Bulgarians had no film industry, they now have a very active one. The films that interest the directors are those with human significance. Such a film is *Stars,* made a few years ago jointly by Bulgarian and East German studios. It concerns a trainload of Jews, during World War II, being taken from Greece through Bulgaria on the way to a German death camp. One of the German guards falls in love with one of the Jewish girls, and this brings about a great change in him. The story, however, ends tragically: the train does go through.

"We Bulgarians," said Mr. Belogorski, "are very tolerant, perhaps the least discriminatory people on earth. In this film there is an internationalism which is one of our inherent qualities. That's why we make a lot of films not only about our country but about our international spirit. We are sorry we haven't the power to present this international spirit so well that it will capture the imagination of people everywhere. Our main theme is the contemporary scene. As background, we like to tell about our history, about our struggle against the Turkish yoke, and about the 1923 anti-fascist uprising—the first in the world."

He was at the time working on a documentary film in color on Bulgaria's cooperative relations with other countries. It starts with Syria, where Bulgarian engineers and supervisory personnel were building two complete hydroelectric stations. It shows that country of ruined civilizations, the desert, then the people on the construction project bringing water and life. Next, the film goes to Tunisia, where Bulgarian architects and engineers have won a contest to rebuild the center of Tunis. Two contrasting ideas are presented: the city exploited and ruined by colonialism; and the city now being reconstructed with the help of the Bulgarians—whose country is also newly developing but at a more advanced stage. The scene then shifts to Algiers, where Bulgarian architects and engineers are building a hospital which is to be equipped and staffed by Bulgarians. The two final episodes present the Bulgarian exhibits at two international fairs—in Vienna and Moscow. These show "not only tomatoes and peppers," but also Bulgarian industrial and cultural achievements.

In 1963 Mr. Belogorski made a documentary color film called *On the Roads of Africa,* presenting the newly liberated nations there. The first country to buy this film was—West Germany! The Germans commented that they were "tired of looking at jungles and tigers," and wanted "to know something about the people of Africa, how these people are going to live from now on, and how they are going to use the new freedom that they have."

"In making this film," Mr. Belogorski said, "we didn't have West Germany in mind; it was intended mainly to show to our own people."

The talk turned to how Bulgarians feel about their life and

their work today. "We are happy here," he said, "because we are not very rich. If we were rich, we would not be happy.

"There is a feeling of security in our socialist society," he added. "You can receive a pension after you have worked twenty or twenty-five years. A writer, for example, can retire at about fifty on a pension and then continue to write for many years, without financial worry. His sense of security comes also from the knowledge that he can receive medical and hospital care free of charge, and that his children will get an education. About 80 per cent of his salary is paid him as a pension.

"If you have this security," he said, "you can work better and create better."

Back in Sofia, at supper at a friend's apartment, we met a Bulgarian architect, Hristo Zlatev. He is a hearty, self-confident young man, in the thick of city-planning activities. I asked him his views on the rather severe, monumental architecture of the Hotel Balkan, the Tsum Department Store, and the Communist Party Building, which had been built about 1954 in the center of Sofia.

He replied that Bulgarian architects have made many mistakes, and have also had many successes. Ten years ago they were influenced mainly by the architecture of the U.S.S.R.

"Has there been in recent years," my wife asked, "a conscious attempt to make buildings lighter, more varied, and more suited to a southern climate?"

"Yes. Many Bulgarian architects have been traveling abroad recently, and have been reading architectural journals from many countries, both West and East."

In 1960 two Bulgarian architects, working together, won the second prize in a competition for a large building in Bagdad. In 1961 a larger team won a prize in an international competition for the reconstruction of part of Tunis. In 1963, in an international competition for the city of Sofia, a big team of Bulgarian architects won the second and third prizes. (No first prize was awarded.)

Bulgarians are building schools, hospitals, hydroelectric plants, etc., in the Near East and in Africa—Senegal, Syria, Egypt, Iraq, Mali, Guinea, and elsewhere.

I mentioned the modern Zaimov Housing Project in Sofia which I had seen—a group of five- and nine-story apartment buildings, with a restaurant and a theater. Mr. Zlatev commented: "It was built in 1958, and for us that is already old. In the newer housing projects the windows are larger, and modern shops and schools are incorporated. And we are including a lot of balconies now. Sweden has been an example for us."

For the past twelve years he has been working with a team of architects, engineers, and technicians in Sofia on plans for the city and suburbs. There is a council of older architects who make the final decisions. "This is an excellent training school for our young architects," he commented. "Most of our best modern buildings are designed by architects in their thirties. And we have many foreign students of architecture here."

Two things, he said, have greatly influenced Bulgarian architects: sound traditions and new freedoms. There was an excellent artistic tradition in some of their domestic architecture of one hundred to two hundred years ago; and now there are some very competent professors who have inherited these traditions and who are also assimilating the best in foreign countries. There is enthusiasm, too, among the younger generation of architects; they find that their sound, and even bold, imaginative ideas can get a hearing.

Rouzha Staikova, a friend of ours, is a ceramic artist. She is a beaming, generous-hearted, humorous person and a steady campaigner for higher artistic standards. She speaks English fluently; before the war she was a student at the American School in Lovech. Her studio is only a "hole in the wall," behind a battered façade off one of Sofia's main streets. My wife and I made our way between the pottery wheel, the kiln, and a table laden with drying clay shapes to the back of the room. There, instead of a staircase (for there wasn't enough space for one), we saw a ladder. Invited to climb up it, we found ourselves in a small loft, which served as living room, bedroom, dining room, and library. It was full of interesting things: vases and bowls from her pottery wheel, experiments with glazes, plaster casts made from Thracian originals, books in half a dozen languages, and shards of pottery from many centuries and many civilizations, from which she was drawing ideas for her work.

She told us that for a time she had worked as a restorer of ceramics in the Archaeological Museum. One day, officials there showed her a big heap of pottery shards in the cellar of the museum, which they thought they could do nothing with, and said, "Rouzha, have a look at this. Why don't you try your hand and see if you can put some of these pieces together?" She spent several months, off and on, at the task. It was very puzzling at first, and progress was slow; but at the end, she had assembled and put together a number of irreplaceable jugs, platters, and other pieces from ancient epochs. She told us that in this experience her hands became so skilled that, with her eyes shut, she could tell—by feeling the surface, the glaze, and the unglazed material at broken edges—whether a fragment had been made by Greeks, Thracians, Romans, Byzantines, or others.

We learned that some four hundred or five hundred of the artists in Bulgaria—painters, sculptors, ceramic artists, woodcarvers, textile designers, etc.—are members of the Union of Bulgarian Artists. A jury decides which applicants shall be admitted to membership. To be a member carries certain advantages: you get space for a studio assigned to you, and commissions for work—for example, on public buildings, in restoring archaeological treasures, and creating new and better designs for industrial production.

At the 1963 annual exhibition of painting and sculpture, more than four thousand works were submitted, but only three hundred were shown. This is because Sofia's large exhibition hall was bombed and ruined in World War II, and temporarily a much smaller hall had to be used—a former casino in one of the parks. The jury of over twenty members worked for a month to arrive at decisions.

An Art Council within the Union meets twice a week and allocates the available commissions for work. Each contract is signed by the Union, the enterprise for which the work is to be done, and the artist. Payment to the artist is made through the Union.

The Communist Party recently made a proposal that the directors of certain factories should employ artists to help improve the attractiveness and quality of their products. Some plant managers, if left to their own devices, would be content to use whatever ceramic molds, for example, they have on hand. They say: "These molds are still in good condition. Why should we throw them away?"

At luncheon with my wife and me one day, Rouzha Staikova, always enthusiastically devoted to her artistic ideals, could scarcely eat from the durable but plain blue-rimmed white plates in this otherwise excellent restaurant. She vehemently declared that restaurants should be supplied with plates of more artistic and more varied design. She said that as a result of each annual exhibition of artists' work, some changes are made in factory-produced ceramics. But many artists, she among them, have decided to try to exert more influence on factories to produce goods of higher artistic quality.

A writer on Bulgarian history has commented that "there are few countries in the world where the past is so much a part of the present as in Bulgaria." This is true of archaeology as well as of history. For more than two thousand years Bulgaria has been a crossroads for many civilizations; and especially since 1944 many beautiful and strange objects of great artistic interest have been discovered by accident or dug up during organized excavations. One of the curators of the Archaeological Museum in Plovdiv told me that there are an estimated ten thousand Thracian tumuli in Bulgaria, most of them in the valley of the Maritsa River (which flows through Plovdiv), and that most of these have not yet been excavated. Hundreds of such mounds, in which the Thracians may have buried their dead, were destroyed, over the ages, in the process of farming. The peasants "gradually tilled them flat."

I was reminded of a statement made to me by an archaeologist in Mexico, some years ago, that probably not one per cent of the archaeological sites in that country had yet been excavated— largely because of a lack of funds and of archaeologists. But today in Bulgaria considerable funds are being provided by the Government, and many young archaeologists and technical personnel are being trained.

One way in which "the past is so much a part of the present" is in the use of ancient and medieval motifs by contemporary artists and craftsmen. A modern ceramic wine set, consisting of pitcher and little cups, may be based on ancient Greek forms, combined with elements of traditional Bulgarian folk art to give a harmonious and pleasing result.

In the United States, if you are lucky, you may come upon an Indian arrowhead several hundred years old. In Bulgaria— but you have to be quite a bit luckier—you may come upon a Thracian chariot two thousand years old. It was a Thracian custom to bury a rich man's chariot with him. The wheels had iron spokes; the wooden body was strengthened with iron, and the sides and back were decorated with bronze statuettes. During the past several decades, at least eleven such chariots have been found.

The ruins of a Roman town called Abritus, long known to have existed but not previously located in modern times, were discovered in 1953 in northeastern Bulgaria. This ancient town was the site of a fierce battle in 251 A.D., in which the Goths defeated the Romans, though they themselves are said to have lost thirty thousand men. The site was identified by the discovery of an altar there, erected in honor of Hercules, with a Latin inscription mentioning the Roman ruler of those days. Another check on this location was by a map found in a library in Cracow, Poland; it was made in the seventeenth or eighteenth century, from some ancient map. Abritus today, with some of its pillars again standing erect on the broad plain, is an impressive —and a thought-provoking—ruin.

In 1949 three brothers who were digging in clay soil to make the foundation for a house came upon nine drinking vessels of gold. These are of elaborate *repoussé* work, considered to be of Thracian design but following Greek traditions, made in the fourth or third century B.C. I saw them in the Archaeological Museum in Plovdiv. So far as their condition is concerned, they might have been made yesterday. Three of them are in the shape of women's heads, with straight-line "Grecian" noses; the handles are in the form of winged lions with women's heads. Three are deers' heads; one is in the form of a goat; there is a shallow bowl with many heads of Negroes on the bottom; and there is a large goblet with two handles in the form of centaurs.

When discovered, these objects were together, resting on the bowl. No other artifacts were found nearby, nor are any remains of an ancient town known in that vicinity. The generally accepted theory is that this treasure was owned by a rich Thracian who buried it in haste during an invasion and then fled, hoping to come back later and dig it up again. These objects, known as the Golden Treasure of Panagyurishté, have been exhibited in museums in the Soviet Union, Poland, and Paris, and when I saw them were about to be sent for exhibit at the Krupp Gallery in Essen, West Germany.

In 1960 the foundations for a cultural and recreation center for young people were being dug in the town of Sandanski, in southwestern Bulgaria, when workmen came upon a beautiful mosaic floor in many colors. Construction work was stopped; archaeologists from Sofia, together with local museum people, determined that this was the floor of a Byzantine basilica of the fifth or sixth century. The architectural plans for the House of Youth were altered so as to include the mosaic floor, which is carefully preserved for all to see.

One day about four years ago, some workers on a cooperative farm turned up a copper vessel containing 786 gold coins. These had been minted in the reigns of various emperors of the eleventh and twelfth centuries. They had probably been buried by a feudal lord who was forced to flee the country when, in the twelfth century, armies of the Second Bulgarian Kingdom swept down and drove out the Byzantine rulers. Many of these coins show an emperor in royal robes, holding a sceptre in his right hand and an orb in the other. On the reverse side is the head of Christ with a halo, and the inscription: "Lord God, Protect Emperor Comnenus" (or whatever the name was).

In our country, with all our twentieth-century progress, it would seem that in basic attitudes we are not very different from these medieval rulers. Instead of a sceptre, our leaders' symbol of power is Foreign Aid; instead of the orb, the Bomb. And on the reverse side of our coins we still print: "In God We Trust."

CHAPTER 16

CRIME AND PUNISHMENT

Much light is thrown on the character of a government by its laws and by its treatment of those who transgress its laws. Are the procedures arbitrary or democratic? In Bulgaria, does a person convicted of a crime have adequate right of appeal? What, in general, are the punishments for minor, and for major, crimes? Is the emphasis placed on punishment or rehabilitation? What is done to train a prisoner for a normal, constructive life? Does a person who has served a prison term emerge as an outcast? Does he have difficulty finding a job?

It was with such questions as these that my wife and I went to the Ministry of Justice Building in the center of Sofia for an interview with two of the top men in Bulgaria's judicial system. One was Mr. Pencho Spasov, Head of Judicial Supervision of Punishment in the Chief Prosecutor's (Attorney General's) office. The other was Mr. Jeliazko Troiev, Head of the Department of Prison Inspection in the Ministry of Justice.

The Chief Prosecutor, elected by the National Assembly, supervises all the ministries, including the Ministry of Justice, in respect to whether they are carrying out the laws; and he appoints all other public prosecutors.

During the first few years after 1944, Bulgaria, while retaining most of the pre-war laws, eliminated those which were against the new regime. For example, there was a trade law which favored rich merchants; this was abolished. Since the State now conducts foreign trade, practically all previous laws regarding such trade have been rescinded. The same with regard to private industry.

"First of all," said Mr. Spasov, "the legal procedures had to be made more democratic, because the basis of the new Constitution is that the Government derives its powers from the people and belongs to the people. Before 1944, all judges were appointed. But now lower court judges are elected. And we have introduced legal advisers (they are not necessarily lawyers) in court cases. The Ministry of Justice has a list of all practicing lawyers, and when there is a vacancy in a judgeship, the Ministry proposes some candidates to the Fatherland Front. Then the Fatherland Front at its public meetings discusses the candidates, and these meetings decide which will be nominated and be voted on in the elections."

The People's Court is the lowest court. If a person is not satisfied with its decision, he may appeal to the next higher court, the District Court. (The judges of the District Court are elected by the People's Councils in the district concerned.) Finally there is the Supreme Court, whose judges are elected by the National Assembly for a five-year term.

The People's Court handles 80 per cent of the cases. The District Court takes appeals, and the most serious cases such as murder, espionage, and treason. And all these may be appealed to the Supreme Court.

The Supreme Court takes appeals from the District Courts. And even a sentence which has twice been confirmed can be challenged again as to its legality by appeal to the Chief Prosecutor as Chairman of the Supreme Court. This provision is a correction of the old principle 'Take as lawful the verdict of the judge," because now a decision can be reviewed for the third time and, if necessary, corrected. "We don't allow a decision to be carried out," said Mr. Spasov, "in which there is the slightest possibility of its not being in accordance with the law."

In a Bulgarian court there are one judge and two advisers. The latter sit one on each side of the judge and have equal right with him to say whether a defendant is guilty, and if so, what punishment he should receive. The court has in mind that the advisers should know something about the defendant, his work, and his reputation. For example, if he is a railroad worker, the court is likely to appoint railroad workers as advisers. The defendant has the right of legal defense, even while the preliminary investigation is going on. He can choose any lawyer he wants, and his lawyer has the right to know all the materials of the preliminary investigation, and to appeal even while the investigation is going on. The appeal must be checked and considered, and answers given to all questions. Mr. Spasov stressed the importance of this provision, adding that in some countries no permission is given for legal defense during the preliminary investigation.

If a defendant doesn't know any lawyer, he can turn to the chairman of the Legal Consultation—a sort of lawyers' cooperative—and have a lawyer appointed for him. If he doesn't have money, he can ask the court or the Legal Consultation to appoint a lawyer to represent him without charge. In a minor case, a defendant may defend himself, but if he is indicted for a very serious crime, legal defense is obligatory.

When a prosecutor introduces a case in court, a copy of the indictment is handed to the defendant, who has the right to have his objections to it considered and to bring proof of his contentions.

Until the trial, a defendant can either be released or held under guard, depending on whether the case is a minor or a serious one, or how dangerous he might be. For the most serious crimes, the accused person has to be kept under guard. For other offenses, a guarantee is arranged—either money or property, or the defendant signs a declaration that he will appear in court.

"As to the kind and amount of punishment," said Mr. Spasov, "we are basically different from many other countries. For a first offense of a minor kind, the person is talked with and criticized by people in the place where he works. A second type of punishment is that the convicted person has his salary or wages reduced. (Not over 25 per cent of it is taken away, and for not over one year.) The next more serious punishment is taking away his freedom. The minimum sentence is one day; the maximum, twenty years. We don't have life imprisonment in Bulgaria."

A person who receives any sentence of from one day to three years may be, if the court so decides, exempted from prison and released on probation, if the crime is a minor one and if it is his first offense.

"We have very few political prisoners," said Mr. Spasov. "Political crimes were a problem immediately after the Revolution, but not any more."

The death penalty is given only for very exceptional, most serious cases, such as treason, espionage, certain kinds of murder cases, and serious offenses against the State, such as large-scale stealing from the Government. The penal code says: either death or twenty years. It depends on the crime and on the decision of the court.

The prisons in Bulgaria are under the Ministry of Justice. Militiamen are used as guards outside a prison, but have no right to go inside. The personnel who see to the discipline inside the prison are supervisors—and they are not armed.

"Not armed?" I asked.

Mr. Troiev, Head of the Department of Prison Inspection, replied, "If a prisoner is physically dangerous, he is put in another part of the prison. If mentally ill, he is put in a mental institution. There has been no case of a prisoner attacking an employee."

Under the Bulgarian Constitution all healthy prisoners have to work. And two days worked are equivalent to three days of the prison sentence. Thus if a man who has a three-year sentence works for two years, he is released at the end of the two years. Every prison has a factory or a farm. The factories make mainly furniture, clothing, shoes, metal work, and bakery products. Those prisoners who have a trade, work at it; the others are required to learn a trade. If, for example, a prisoner is a doctor or an engineer, he is employed as a doctor or engineer in the prison, or teaches courses in prison in his specialty.

"What happens to a man when he is released from prison?" my wife asked.

"For each prison," said Mr. Troiev, "there is a supervisory

commission. It includes the public prosecutor, one of the vice-chairmen of the local People's Council, the top person in education, and a judge. They go to the prison and supervise the work and the conditions there. A month before a prisoner is to be released, the head of the prison must write a letter to the People's Council member of the commission regarding the prisoner's qualifications. And the commission then has the right— in fact, the responsibility—to see to it that, with the help of the People's Council, a job is found for the prisoner into which he can go after his release."

CHAPTER 17

WHAT'S AHEAD?

By now we see that Bulgarians and Americans have many ideas and ideals in common. They and we want an environment that will bring children through a secure and happy childhood to a healthy maturity, both physical and psychological. They and we want jobs for those who can work, and economic security for those who can't or who have worked long enough. They and we want more and better education, more and better housing, and adequate medical care without crippling expense. And, with the Bulgarians, we believe—at least according to an honored American document, we believe—in "certain unalienable rights" for all, regardless of creed or color.

We have seen something of what Bulgarians are doing to achieve these things. Are we doing enough about them over here?

Above all, the Bulgarians and we want peace. But what are *we* doing about peace—realistically? Early in this book I quoted President Johnson: "Today, under the shadows of atomic power, it is not rhetoric but it is truth to say that we must either love each other or we must die." Good. But what is the political and military reality? "U.S. to Enlarge Vietnam Forces by 5,000 Advisers. Total to Be 21,000" (New York *Times*, July 28, 1964).

"We must never relax our efforts," said Albert Einstein as long ago as 1946, "to rouse in the peoples of the world, and especially in their governments, an awareness of the unprecedented disaster which they are absolutely certain to bring on themselves unless there is a fundamental change in their attitude toward one another . . . The unleashed power of the atom has changed everything except our ways of thinking."

In Bulgaria, war propaganda is forbidden by law. Bulgarians

know that a third world war would destroy their dreams, their achievements, and themselves. They have had much more experience of the brutality and devastation of war than most Americans. They and their Government are for general and total disarmament under strict international supervision. As one step toward peace they favor a non-aggression pact between the NATO and the Warsaw Treaty countries.

Bulgaria endorses the Rapacki Plan for a nuclear-weapons-free ("atom-free") zone in Central Europe. The United Nations General Assembly has proposed that the whole of Africa be made atom-free. Five of the largest South American states have urged in the U.N. that the whole of Latin America be declared an atom-free zone. In Northern Europe there is a growing interest in making Scandinavia atom-free.

For some years now, Bulgarians have been working for a ban on all atomic bases in the Balkans. And, they ask, why should not the whole Mediterranean area be made atom-free too? If and when this is done in one area, why not in another—in many others? Then, indeed, the international political climate would become more favorable for achieving general and total disarmament.

This is man's only remaining chance for survival.

A number of important agreements between Bulgaria and Greece were signed in Athens in July, 1964. These include long-term agreements on trade; the developing and sharing of water resources of rivers that flow through the territory of both countries; flood control; improved inter-country transportation by road, railroad, ship and plane; telegraph and telephone communication; expanded tourism between the two countries; and a large program of scientific and cultural cooperation, with exchange of students, scholars, writers, artists, composers, and others.

These agreements provide also that the two countries shall use only peaceful means for solving any question between them and shall permanently give up all territorial claims against each other.

The joint communiqué states that this new cooperation "provides a strong basis for preserving peace in the Balkans and the world."

"The settlement of these vast and complicated questions," said the Bulgarian Minister of Foreign Affairs, Ivan Bashev, "has shown that, with good will and a realistic approach, even the most difficult issues can be solved between two countries with different political systems."

R
U
M
A

Vidin

Danube

Mikhailovgrad

Pleven

Vratsa

Lovech

Isker R.

Gabrov

Sofia

Koprivshtitsa

P

L

Panagyurishté

Karlovo

Hissar-Momina
Banya

Isker Dam

Kyustendil

Borovets

Plovdiv

Rila Monastery

Marits

R I L A

Struma R.

Blagoevgrad

Velingrad

Batak

R
H
O

P I R I N

Gotsé Delchev

Smolyan

Sandanski

Petrich

E
E

P

Y
U
G
O
S
L
A
V
I
A

R

G

E
E

S
T
A